Too Soon Old—
Too Late Smart

Too Soon Old—
Too Late Smart

A Book of Hope and Renewal

Alana L. Lilly

iUniverse, Inc.
New York Lincoln Shanghai

Too Soon Old—Too Late Smart
A Book of Hope and Renewal

iUniverse books may be ordered through booksellers or by contacting:

iUniverse
2021 Pine Lake Road, Suite 100
Lincoln, NE 68512
www.iuniverse.com
1-800-Authors (1-800-288-4677)

ISBN-13: 978-0-595-38787-8 (pbk)
ISBN-13: 978-0-595-83167-8 (ebk)
ISBN-10: 0-595-38787-X (pbk)
ISBN-10: 0-595-83167-2 (ebk)

Printed in the United States of America

♍ Dedication ♎

My Husband

This book I dedicate to the memory of my late husband, Richard L. Lilly (August 25, 1934–April 12, 2005). There is such a void in our lives since you left. We miss you and love you so much.

My Parents

I honor my father, Edward Harold Pross (1918–1969) who, in his deepest despair, chose to end his life by suicide. *Daddy, that wasn't the answer.*

♍♎

The title of this book gives tribute to my wonderful mother, Juanita F. Pross, to whom I owe the distinguished honor and privilege of being her daughter.

My Friend

Keri Amanda Tyre (March 30, 1984–March 30, 2003), the belated beautiful daughter of one of my friends, Melinda Tyre.

♍ Contents ♎

♍ Acknowledgement ♎

I thank Deborah White. Without your computer knowledge and fitting me into your schedule time and time again, the completion of this book would not have been possible. Thanks from the bottom of my heart.

♍ Introduction ♎

For the last several months, a thought has kept popping up in my mind: write a book. Of course, wouldn't we all love that idea to do that? Write a book, be famous, and make lots of money. Fairy tale stuff, right? Thinking *our* story would make an impact on someone else's life? Get real! Our lives aren't fiction. Our lives are very real. So, I would push the idea aside and continue on with my daily routine. Hours would go by or maybe a few days, then again, the thought would creep up: write a book. I'd say to myself, Lord, are you trying to tell me something? What would I say in this book? Again, I shoved the idea away from my thought process.

I'm a Christian. And heaven knows, I haven't been going to church on a regular basis. I have, however, started to get involved again. I have joined a church recently that I feel quite at home with. The people are warm and welcoming and, the pastor is, a God-fearing man. I'm not a Sunday school teacher. I tell myself I will tithe better. I set goals for myself to do this or that concerning the church. I fall so short all the time.

It seems like the little red man sits on my shoulder, giving me negative vibes more than I care to admit. I find myself constantly saying, "get thee behind me, Satan." Write a *book*? I don't think so. Besides, I don't know the first thing about composing a book. Let alone getting it published. On with the daily stuff I go, ignoring the idea completely.

When God wants us to do something, He is very stubborn and won't let it rest. Most days I try to take a few minutes, sit down with a cup of coffee or a cold drink at my computer desk, and read my incoming e-mails. When checking my junk mail, I usually scan it briefly, and then, click delete. Low and behold, there is one that jumps out at me: *"Thinking about writing a book?"* Check out Tate Publishing, a Christian publishing company. Ok. This is getting creepy!

During this past 2005 Christmas holidays, I spent a few relaxing days in the mountains of Blowing Rock, North Carolina, at Maple Lodge. During that stay, I met a wonderful Christian couple from Durham, North Carolina. We had breakfast one morning. Somewhere in the midst of conversation, he mentioned that he worked for Core Publishing and was promoting an idea for a new magazine.

That crazy idea hit me again. *Write a book.* I felt like Tom Hanks in the movie, *Forrest Gump*, when the main female character, his friend Jenny, kept saying; "Run, Forest, run!" "Write a book! Write a book!" just kept running through my brain like water running out of a faucet. I still had no idea what to write, or how to begin, or what I was supposed to say to make a difference.

One of my biggest concerns was that I had absolutely no training in journalism and no professional experience in publishing. I kept reminding God over and over again of this very important issue. The Lord kept at me, saying, "Keep telling your readers of the importance of this book and how it will impact the lives of other women out there." He kept assuring me everything would be ok. "Just write the book. Let the words flow from your heart. Your experiences and passion will offset any lack of credentials."

I wish for each of you joy, inner peace, and faith to define your living and your life, and love and compassion to make the rest worthwhile. It is my sincere desire that these words I write will bring a little smile to your day......, some hope for your tomorrow......, and maybe perhaps a tear sliding down your cheek from your eye to humble you and help you hang on when the storms blow through.

Sincerely,
Alana L. Lilly

1

♍ Youth: Oh, My Goodness, Youth ♎

My early childhood up through the teenage years and until I left home was, in my mind, relatively normal. I am what they call a "baby-boomer,"—that which means I was born shortly after World War II.

Barbara Johnson writes a lot of spiritual sayings, and I'll use one of her phrases: "According to my birth certificate I'm somewhere between estrogen and death," or as someone else said, "…between menopause and LARGE PRINT."

I grew up in the era of Elvis Presley, bobby socks, and saddle shoes. For entertainment, we went to sock hops. For you, who do not know, what "bobby socks" are, they're were solid white socks that were folded down to the ankle and worn with the black-and-white saddle shoes. At my high school in Knoxville, Tennessee, girls could not wear jeans; they had to wear skirts or dresses to school. The boys had to wear nice pants or nice jeans, and their shirts had to be tucked in with a belt.

Getting pregnant and continuing to attend school was unheard of. Teenage pregnancies and unwed pregnancies outside of marriage were always hushed. And when it did happen, off the girl would go until the baby was born. Usually, her reputation ruined if word did get out. Abortions were not legal.

Teenagers hung out at the local drug store or hamburger joint where they feasted on RC Cola and moon pies, French fries and a juicy hamburger. RC stood for Royal Crown Cola, a popular soft drink. The RC brand is less popular today, but the company still exists. Old habits are hard to break. To this day, I still buy a twelve-12 pack of RC and keep them in my refrigerator.

When our parents said, "No," it meant "No". Fear and respect just went hand in hand where they were concerned. It was a totally different era than what you see in today's teenagers. Pot was something you cooked in. Weed was an unwanted plant that you pulled out of the garden. Crack was a broken part in a plate. The boys had a designated smoking area behind the schools. Only "loose" girls smoked. Now everywhere is a smoke-free environment.

We laughed, teased our siblings, lied, snuck out, got caught, were grounded, and I mean grounded! We had slumber parties that were strictly for girls. We spent the night rolling our hair on huge rollers or used an iron and ironing board to straighten our hair. Yes, you read it correctly—I did say "iron". I have natural curly hair and used to iron it to straighten it. Of course, the minute it would rain, or when there was the least bit of humidity, *poof*—curly locks again! Always trying to change what the good Lord gives us. Never satisfied.

My mother was the solid foundation of our home. She also was a wonderful seamstress. The beautiful gowns she used to make me were perfect. It wasn't until years later, that I really came to appreciate the hours upon hours she put into those beautiful dresses and gorgeous gowns. She could scold, spank, and send me to my room. Then the next minute she would be up there defending me, speaking her mind. Which, by the way, she did numerous times.

I am so blessed to have entered the world through my mother. To have spent my formative years in her love, and tenderness, and tutoring in the basic principals of life. I am honored to have received from my mother the groundwork which gave me the strength to weather the life challenges I faced.

Because of his job, my father was gone a lot, and my mother held the household together. Because of my dad's career as a civil engineer, we were transferred frequently. I was fortunate to have lived in many states growing up. Living in different places like that was a wonderful learning experience. It is the basis of some of my fondest memories. One of my happiest experiences was living in Toronto, Canada, for nearly eight years. My father helped construct the Saint Lawrence Seaway. The details of this nearly eight-year project was so news worthy, that it made the cover of *Times* Magazine.

Close to my teens, we were transferred to Tennessee where my immediate family is to this day. I guess you could say it is where I planted my roots. They call me a transplanted southerner.

As some people age, they grow nostalgic for yesteryear. Not me. There was just too much stress, tragedy, and sadness. The worst moment was when my father committed suicide. I was only twenty-two years old at the time-22. This was such a tremendous and unnecessary waste. He was a brilliant man, but an alcoholic. He would attend Alcoholics Anonymous, then stop at the local liquor store and pick up a bottle of Vodka on the way home. Alcoholism—the disease is a killer. It took my father's life.

Then came Vietnam. And next the body bags. I would bet that I lost one third of my male friends—guys I went to high school with or associated with during that time frame. They left for Vietnam, and never came home! As the guys would prepare to leave to fight in the war, we would have heart-wrenching good-byes. All of us gathering at the airport, along with our parents, with tears streaming down our faces, hoping and praying we would set eyes on them again. These were boys we had giggled with, given secret kisses, danced with, defied school rules with by holding hands while walking down the hallways, and had long phone conversations that tied up the telephone lines until our mom's would yell, "Get off the phone!" Watching them leave tore us apart.

I did a lot of stupid things and repeated the same dumb mistakes while life kept kicking my butt until I came to my senses. A lot of coming to my senses was getting pregnant as a teenager. There was no reason for this to have happened. I just flat ignored all the sensible sex education conversations mom and I had.

I was only sixteen years old. Much to my mother's dismay, my steady boyfriend was a few years older than I was. He had just recently gotten discharged from the Navy and was so good-looking. I guess there's a reason why parents tell you not to do something, but at sixteen, it's very easy to confuse lust and love. I was far too young to understand the depth of commitment and responsibility, and the consequences that follow poor decisions.

The days between when I realized I had missed my period and when I finally had to tell my mother were torture. It was bad. Really bad. I mean, how do you start the conversation? "Mom, guess what?" No, that doesn't sound right. "Mom, I haven't had a period this month. Do you think anything's wrong?" It only took my mother two seconds to figure it out, and another two seconds to call the doctor. Oh, she was so mad at me. Maybe mad is not the right word.—it was more that she was disappointed and hurt. She had been trying to tell me, protect me.

Back in those days, parents didn't explain why you shouldn't do something, they just told the girls, "Don't do it. Wait until you get married. The right guy will come along, and you will just know." They told the boys, "Make sure you don't get those girls pregnant "'cause you're going to have to marry them." Contradiction? Yes, but that was life in the sixties.

And if getting pregnant wasn't bad enough, then I decided to run away and get married right after high school. I didn't actually decide to just get married, it was more of a spur-of-the-moment thing that my steady boyfriend, at that time, thought we would do.

Here's what happened. We took another couple to Ringgold, Georgia, to get married. My steady boyfriend was a freshman at the University of Tennessee, and he had a car. So we drove them to Ringgold to find the local Justice of the Peace. I can't remember exactly what happened. I think it might have been that my girl-friend wasn't old enough. So there we were. In Ringgold and in love. So believe it or not, my steady boyfriend and I got married. Our marriage lasted six years and included the birth of a daughter.

Life is a see-saw. Up and down, down and up. God has always foreseen what I needed for my life. Even though I refused to listen, I went directly against His wishes. I'd fall, get hurt, and get myself in a mess. He would pick me back up again, dust me off, and start me out all over again. My path to what I have become today was made with detours, ruts, and trenches. At the same time, it has been a wonderful journey, full of laughter, tears, love, losses, and gains: loss of a father and, gain of a beautiful daughter whom my dad never met.

There I was with all of my dysfunction. I was twenty-two years old with a husband and a baby. I had endured challenges that would make your head spin. It was nothing short of a miracle that we held our marriage together for six years. And it was surprising to me that mother and daughter survived at all.

It is simply by the grace of God that she still calls me mother. Trying to raise a daughter alone, hold down a job, was overwhelming. I soon realized that I didn't have patience and discipline to be the kind of mother that my own mother had been. As my daughter grew up, our relationship became dangerous and harrowing—to the point of hatred.

2

♍ As the Beat Goes On ♎

I don't know a person who has avoided making an unwise, uninformed, or unscrupulous decision. Sure, some of these decisions can not be undone, we must live with them. There are consequences to everything we do or say. During my growing up formative years, I was always in church or at some church activity. Oh, isn't it interesting how youth can often miss the point entirely? There is a huge difference between worshipping God and showing off. I have been baptized, sprinkled on, and dunked. I got down on my knees at many an altar and swore to our Jesus that I would do better, walk the narrow path. I accepted Jesus as my savior and reaffirmed my faith numerous times.

As young adults, we think we will live forever. Our earthly parents have patience, most of the time, for our foolish acts and mannerisms. But, God through the ages keeps on being patient. He lets us act like a fool and sometimes lets us really get in a situation to wake us up. Whether it is a car accident or an injury of some sort or, maybe something even scares us to death before something *almost* happens. At times, He even takes one of His youth *home* to save them from something down the road unbeknown to us. So as I continued through my stages, I still failed to grasp the significance of life, honor, and marriage.

Turning your life 100% over to Jesus. Appreciation for parents, the word "respect". I could go on and on. My mother has a saying that she has used many, many times, "Too soon old, too late smart.",", a Germanic folk saying. It has taken years for those six, short words to make any sense to me. And guess what? More than half of my life is gone! That is, if heredity is on my side, and I live to be at least the age of my mother, who just turned 80. That gives me twenty-five more years. Wake up call!

A few weeks ago, I read something in of one of those little inspirational books. It really got my attention. It was something about a theory of "a thousand marbles." This person said that at age fifty-five, he began to realize his weeks and years were flying by. He figured that the average person might live to be 75 years old. And with 52 weeks in a year, that gave him approximately 1,000 precious weekends with the people he loved. So he purchased 1,000 marbles, put them in a clear container, and placed it on his desk. Every Monday he would take one marble out and throw it away. As the marbles diminished, he focused more on being what God would like him to be. Guess there is nothing like watching your time on earth running out to get your priorities straight.

Have you ever wondered just why it takes so long for most of us to come to our senses? By His grace we wake up each morning to face another day regardless of whether or not we have done what God has required of us. Jesus never said life would be easy.

In 1 Peter 3:12 says, "The eyes of the Lord watch over those who do right, and His ears are open to their prayers." In Philippians 4:13 says, "I can do all things through Christ that strengthens me." For those of us who goof up, God is still there to love, guide, and give strength. I have a firm belief that: whatever doesn't kill you makes you stronger.

Your success or failure in life will not be decided by the number of setbacks you encounter, but, rather, how you react to them. We cannot change our past mess up's, nor can we change the fact that people will act in a certain way. We can not control gossip. We cannot change the inevitable. We can only play with the one life line we have: faith. God's promise to help is genuine.

Our lives can be hectic. I know mine is. We get caught up with our cell phones, house phones, work schedules, school schedules, and children's sports—…you name it. I lose sight of what is important, don't you? I get rushed, short tempered, and tired. Then the day is over, and God gives me another twenty-four hours and, another extension to do His will. He gave me another day to be with the people I love, and you know what? I didn't give God the time of day.

I could kick myself when I do that! Just as communicating with our spouse, kids, and friends is critical to the health of those relationships, communicating with God is just as vital.

The more time I spend with God, the more clearly I'll see through His eyes. I know that a few minutes with my Lord can recharge my emotional battery to give me courage and the energy to meet another day's hectic rat race. God might not change your situation, but it always transforms the way I view it and react to it. It's a lot like, you know, like taking our parents for granted until we no longer have them.

I can not tell you how many times since my dad's death that I have yearned for his presence. His selfish act of taking his life has left so many questions unanswered. So, of course, that makes my mom more precious. Having said that, do I tell her how much I love her on a daily basis? No. We live in two different states,—me—in North Carolina and my mother in Tennessee—but we talk frequently.

Does she really know how I feel about her and how much she means to me? I'm sure she does. I need to tell her more often. So, it is with our Lord in heaven. He needs to know just how much He is loved and appreciated. I fall so short of that.

3

♍ Keep on Trucking' ♎

Even with passion and purpose in our lives, we are all faced with hardships. There are many roadblocks, detours, and potholes. People are faced with setbacks. Life can be hard and grossly unfair. Have you ever felt that perhaps God had you mixed up with someone else when He said, "I'll never give you more then you can handle?" I'd look up and say, "Lord, please, I can not handle anymore."! Can anyone relate to this? I sure can.

Too many times in my own life, I just wanted to throw up my hands and say, "Okay, I can't take this. I quit." Come on, people, and raise your hands out there if you agree with me. That's better. I was beginning to worry that I was the only one person that had courage that wanes and a heart that doubts. It takes courage and strength to persevere, to hang on while the storms blow through.

Did you know that Walt Disney, despite having declared bankruptcy five times, never gave up? Helen Keller had every reason to feel sorry for herself. Ray Kroc, the founder of McDonalds, was in his 50's and was turned down dozens of times about his hamburger theory, until he found someone to back him financially.

However, Abraham Lincoln was, by far, the man that got my attention. When I want to feel sorry for myself and want to quit, I think of this past President. His setbacks were devastating, to say the least. He failed in business in 1831. He was defeated for state legislature in 1832. He started another business venture in 1833. It failed. His fiancée died in 1835. He was so hurt and grieving he had a nervous breakdown in 1836. In 1843 he ran for Congress and was defeated. He tried in 1848 and was again defeated! He tried running for the Senate in 1855 and, bless his heart, did not make it. Ran for vice president and didn't win. Finally, in 1860 he ran for president, and everyone knows from history he won.

He didn't know what quit was."! I swear, if it were me, I would have probably thrown in the towel. Giving up was not an option for him. When you study and read about his life, you can honestly feel his pain—or I could, anyway. My heart bled for him. It takes guts, determination, will-power, and a lot of stubbornness, but last, but not least, it takes faith to get through those troubled waters that life throws our way.

R. Turnball says, "Beautiful light is born of darkness, so the faith that springs from conflict is often the strongest and best." This has to happen. If not, and you aren't really careful, you become cynical, and bitter, and full of hatred. You then start your violin, and are playing, "woe is me, and woe is me. Let's feel sorry for me." Listen, it is human, to do just that, to feel sorry for us-ourselves. I can't believe Abe didn't have "his feel sorry for me moments". But, the point is, don't give up and quit.

Other people have shown such strength and courage. And I don't understand why my father couldn't have done the same thing. That is what has bugged me for years about my father's suicide. The devil won.

My father's courage was down. He was as low as he could get…. All negative thoughts. Attitude headed in the wrong direction…anger and resentment setting in…. Then boom! The devil strikes and my father is dead of a self-inflicted gun shot wound right through his chest. He is dead and the devil had the last laugh. Not like the song "Devil Went Down to Georgia." The dark side wins and the devil himself chalks one up.

Over the past 40 years, I've experienced many peaks and valley, felt depressed and very down in the dumps. Sometimes I've wanted to close myself in a closet and hide. There have been other times when I even contemplated taking my life. But, I ran like heck in the other way, to God's arms, and He points me in the direction of counselors, friends, family, and churches.

My father's death has haunted me throughout the years. The pain, loneliness and life's tragedies have been enough to bring me to my knees, screaming for help. I didn't have the strength and the wisdom to fight the battles alone. "All things are possible to him who believes." (Mark 9:23). Are you listening out there?

I am human and have blood running through my veins like the rest of you. I've made mistakes. I've been selfish. I turned away from church and going to church. I've gone months on end without giving God a glance, let alone, a prayer. And, yet I'm still here. Why? Because my Lord and Jesus Christ loves me, and I guess He isn't through with me on earth. Or on the humorous side, maybe, He *is* through with me and keeps letting me stay on this imperfect planet we live in to punish me forever.

Joking aside, God has plans for me. I just don't know what they are yet. I know from the bottom of my heart, He wants me to write this book.

And as for you, well, you are going to have fears and self-doubt. The question is not *if* you are going to have fears, pains, and tragedy. All of us know that we will. So instead, the question is how will you react to your difficulties and to whom will you turn? Do you turn to the devil, like my father did, and let him win? Or do you turn to God's arms and to family and friends? The love from your family and friends, and your faith in your church family will determine your true success in life.

4

♍ Age: a State of Mind ♎

Age gets a bad name in our society, but we don't have to buy it. Moses lived to be well over 100 years old. And as for me, I'm not quite 100.

For many years, I was a make-up and clothing professional.

One very important tad-bit of knowledge I would like to pass on for future reference for you girls: less is definitely more after forty. God gave each and every one of you a natural beauty. What matters is not your outer appearance. It is what is on the inside that counts.

That doesn't mean you should go around looking like slobs, either. That would be misusing what the good Lord gave us. The styling of your hair, the jewelry you wear, or the cut of your clothes is not as important as inner disposition. Cultivate inner beauty, the gentle, gracious kind, the kind that God delights in. Although we are all made in God's image, not one of us is exactly alike.

It has taken me years and several not-so-wonderful relationships with the opposite sex to realize that my body is God's temple. So women out there: be proud of it. Take care of it. It is the only one you've got. Charm can mislead, and outer beauty fades. The woman to be admired and praised is the woman who lives in the fear of God.

I feel healthier, sexier, wiser, smarter, and more optimistic than I ever have in my life! I'm proud of the way I have turned out—a lot of it can be attributed to genetics. My mother is still a very beautiful woman, inside and out.

Have you ever noticed God allowed a lot of people in the Old Testament to live to be a ripe old age? Why? Believe me; it wasn't because of diet or joining a health club. Maybe it was because God was held in reverence and was obeyed more.

That brings me back to Moses. He was the epitome of an obedient worker. He was in the wilderness over forty years before God sent him on another mission. God was proud of Moses and gave him a long productive life.

I, as just one woman, try to do my part. I wear a bracelet that says, "One nation under God." I have bumper stickers on my SUV, proclaiming my belief in God and country. I am behind our military men and women. We live in the 21st century and we have computers and so much knowledge at our fingertips. I, also, believe that is, again, the purpose in this book. What better way to be heard, hey? My self-confidence has blossomed. I feel like I'm finally becoming who I really am. The beauty that counts is the glow of confidence, the absolute right for self-determination.

I read an article recently that more women over the age of forty are starting something exciting and new in their lives: a business venture, an attempt to write a book, or a pursuit of a college education. In a *More* magazine, I read an article about a woman who was divorced, working as a nurse's aid, and couldn't pay the bills. Sound familiar? She went back to college at 40 to become a doctor! People told her she would be old before she got through. She told them she would be 50 anyway, what did she have to lose?

Plus, hello out there! When did 50 become old? I am 59 and it is my turn to have braces! The kids have had theirs, and it is my turn.

I was diagnosed with osteoporosis a few years ago. I am petite, small framed, and Caucasian. Yes, I am a prime candidate for osteoporosis, internet scams, real estate scams…you name it! But ghee, give me credit for having learned something from my 50 years of living on this planet!

I was speaking one day with a lawyer who was handling some affairs for me. He was trying to persuade me to do something I was entirely against. In fact, he was literally forcing me against my will and giving me ultimatums. I asked to be given one reason I had to do this certain thing.

Are you ready for this? He told me, on the outside I might not look my age, but on the inside, I had, "rickety old bones". For one thing, that is discrimination. The kicker is; this lawyer is 80 and still practicing law. It took everything I had not to get up, reach over, and smack him up the side the head.

Women have more confidence, connections, tolerance.—and when we are backed in a corner we come out fighting. Believe me, I came out fighting! I'm a very hyper lady. I think I have more energy than ten women. At times, it can go against me because I have a hard time relaxing. And then I spend once a week on a massage table for them to get the tension out of my neck and shoulders. My massage therapist swears my shoulders are around my ears when I come in.

Do I believe prayer is a link to stability, sanity, and longevity? Absolutely! Moses had something going with God. There is nothing quite like throwing your hands up and screaming, "God, help me. I can't take this!" He looks down at you, smiles and says to Himself, "Guess that lawyer got her attention, and she needs me." I wait for the last minute, get disgusted and then holler for Him. He knows when we need time in His presence. He helps me put my heart back in rhythm and helps my mind to stop gyrating.

I believe you accumulate years to give you license to be who you want to be. Our culture is youth obsessed. I guess as you grow more mature, you learn that success with whatever you are striving for comes from inside. And what you've accomplished so far is pretty remarkable-, whether it has been a marvelous career outside the house or being that terrific domestic engineer who has been there for your children and your husband.

Another thing, ladies. Quitting work outside the home doesn't mean you quit learning. It is just lovely getting older. You can never tell about life, even with the sorrow and pain; I enjoy being alive very much. I think at my age self-doubt belongs to when I was younger. I have learned to just be happy. I can now create my tomorrows by what I dream today.

Wish upon a star, knowing that God has a plan for the future, for every tomorrow of your life and beyond. That will give you hope that even in your most inadequate moments, the Lord still reigns over your life.

Women are capable of great understanding, great compassion, and great mercy. It seems as if our moods and emotions are a curse rather then a blessing. Some days our emotions seem out of control. We cry easily because we feel for one another. As I have matured, I have come to realize one very important thing: God gave women a commission for which they are perfectly suited.

Several years ago a friend gave me a book called *100 Things I am not going To Do Now That I am 50*. The author, Wendy R. Crisp, did a great job with the book. It is full of quotes and anecdotes. Some of them are hilarious and some are just true and down to earth. I recommend you getting it. This is from one of my favorite sections in her book:

I'm not going to:

1 feign an interest in spectator sport
2 stifle the giggles
3 devalue housework
4 graciously share my grandchildren
5 suffer gadgetry intimidation
6 neglect friends
7 bargain with God
8 wear a plastic raincoat
9 have a joint checking account
10 answer the phone just because it's ringing

...And here are some more good ones:

1 gossip
2 fight back tears
3 get even
4 apologize for memory lapses
5 dwell in the past

Perhaps some of you are like me: in the sort-of autumn of your life, the second half, if we live to be 100. Spring now seems a millennium away, summer has gone too quickly and autumn is upon you. But watch out, world! The swirling, twirling, joint aching, hot flashing, joy-shouting woman is on the loose. Come join me!

5

♍ Music ♎

One of the things I have found that gives me that up-lift I need is music. There are things out there that make us feel better, and music is one of those things.

Many things can help make you feel good and relieve tension. Those are motivational tapes, a good book, laughing, and even crying.

But one of the oldest forms of relief is music. It has its origins in the Bible. Music, at the original Creation, was found in Job 38:7. The first recorded singing on Earth was found in Exodus 15:1. And 1 Samuel 16:23 tell us that music: "refreshes, and drives away evil spirit."

Some of the instruments mentioned in the Bible are cornet, cymbal, dulcimer, flute, harp, organ, pipe, and trumpet. In II Samuel 19:35, Samuel says, "I am this day fourscore years old…can I hear anymore the voice of singing men and singing women?"

Do you suppose that is why, to this day, we liked to have *Happy Birthday* sung to us? In Ecclesiastics 2:8, I gather men singers and women singers and musical instruments. "In Psalms 98:1 "O, sing unto the Lord a new song, let us make joyful noise to rock our salvation." Psalms 104:33, "I will sing unto the Lord as long as I live, I will sing praise to my God while I have my being."

I read somewhere that you should list the twelve songs you like the best, burn them on a CD. Make two copies so you can keep one in your car and the other in your home (or even at work). You should play them when you need that special lift to make your spirits soar.

I personally like country-western music and the oldies songs. There are so many out there to choose from. *The Wind Beneath My Wings* by Bette Midler, *I Hope You Dance* by Lee Ann Womack, *My Give A Damn Is Busted* by Jo Dee Messina, and Dolly Parton's, *Coat of Many Colors,*—which, by the way, is a true story. Dolly's mother did make her that coat of many colors.

From the soundtrack of the movie *Ghost* there are songs like *Ditto, Sam, Molly,* and Conway Twitty's, *Happy Birthday, Darling.* I like Lee Greenwood's *God Bless the USA.* Michael Bolton's music is wonderful! I get teary-eyed when I hear religious songs like *Amazing Grace, Rock of Ages, In the Sweet By and By, Blessed*

Assurance, What a Friend We Have in Jesus, and *I Can Only Imagine.* And, oh, how can I forget Vince Gill's *Go Rest High on That Mountain. Then there is that* song about the devil and God, *The Devil and Johnny Walker.*

Now, getting back to the burn your own CD comment: each of you has a personal preference for music. Choose what *you* like. And as you use this "personalized" CD idea, use it sparingly. Use it only when you feel like you need it, or it will loose its effect. So, have fun searching and burning a CD. Then pop it in. Turn it up. And soar!

6

♍ Laughing So Hard You're Leaning Over & About to Bust ♎

Have you ever laughed so hard, you just couldn't stop? Laugh loud and laugh often. It will keep you healthy, and it will keep your attitude headed in a good direction. Laughter is to the soul what chicken noodle soup is to your body. In fact, I heard that researchers are studying the effects of laughter and the effects of keeping a positive attitude to ward off negative thoughts and relieve tension.

The ole' saying, "I didn't know whether to laugh or cry" is so true. Those two emotions are so closely linked. For example, in Ecclesiastics 3:4 the Bible says, "…a time to weep, a time to laugh; a time to mourn, and a time to dance." In Psalms 2:4 it actually says "He who sits in heaven will laugh." In Luke 6:21, "Blessed are you who hunger now, for you shall be filled. Blessed are you who weep now, for you shall laugh."

The Lord does not like to see us struggle and go through the messes we put ourselves through. There is laughter all around us. I used to love to watch *I Love Lucy*. Lucille Ball was notorious for getting herself in trouble and creating a hilarious comeback that would leave you laughing so hard you would almost pee in your pants.

Comedians have such a God-given gift to stand up and make thousands of people bend over in laughter. Red Skeleton is another one of my favorite comedians. And then there was Bob Hope. He had a gift that was used time and time again to bring laughter and joy to our military service members who were stationed overseas. Other well-known comedians include Phyllis Diller, Jack Benny, Eddie Murphy, and the great comedy team, The Three Stooges.

The earth laughs in flowers. Did you know that? Ralph Waldo Emerson said, "Laughing at you is even better." Have you ever done something and tell yourself, "This is the nuttiest thing I've ever done." And then you crack up at yourself?

A sense of humor is a wonderful gift to have. God knows when we are in overload. Sometimes, laughter is the best anecdote. So, when you are feeling gloomy, get laughing. Put on a funny movie or find something to read. I have always enjoyed *Readers Digest*. It has had, for years, a section of jokes and humorous stories. I would read a couple of those and just laugh for days.

In my household we have a new cocker spaniel. It was a gift to my 14-year-old grandson, Thomas who is like my son in so many ways. He has been with me since he was an infant. In last year's Christmas newsletter, I wrote a little story about our pet:

> ...A little bundle of joy, or should I say, a bundle of "Dennis the Menace" was delivered into Thomas' arms. Their theory was, perhaps, a male figure in Thomas' life would be beneficial. But, this benefit was in the form of a cocoa-colored chocolate, six-week-old, male cocker spaniel. I didn't know whether or not to cry or laugh.
>
> You see, I already have wall-to-wall pets. As most of you know, I am a sucker for animals. Through the ages, we humans try to take control of our own lives and decisions, not letting God have the upper hand. The upper hand, of course, is being this cocker—which, by the way, we were informed to name him "Sir Richard."
>
> Well, Ritchie, as we call him, is quite a character. Being down and depressed isn't an option when you are around him. I heard Thomas laughing one night. When I looked in on him, I noticed his amusement at some weird stunt Ritchie was pulling.
>
> It is a proven fact, that animals have a way of healing. Ritchie is definitely taking his job that the Lord gave him very seriously. He doesn't have a head like most cockers do. Well, I can't say that either. His head is fine; it's his hair that is so different. When you groom cockers, the hair on the top of their heads lies down very smoothly. My other two cockers have no problems. Well, Ritchie, being Ritchie, has this cowlick or a peacock looking hair "thing" that sticks up. It makes him look more like Dennis the Menace, then ever. So when he does his little mischief stuff, he looks at you with this clump of hair "thing" and you crack up.
>
> He has brought us numerous hours of joy. He senses when we are down, and he walks up to you. No, I take that back. Ritchie doesn't walk; he struts. Anyway, he will actually hug you! He will put both of his paws around your neck.
>
> When you put him in his crate at night for "beddie-bye" time, you have to talk to him differently than my other cockers when saying good-night. He doesn't like the dark. He happens to be on the top crate—like the top bunk. If you don't reassure him just right and do

your good-nights just so, he howls this pitiful howl until you go back and do it correctly. Then he curls up and goes to sleep.

Laugh loud, laugh often, it will keep you happy, keep you healthy and keep your attitude positive. Plus, it feels so good!

7

♍ Prayer ♎

In Webster's dictionary, the definition of prayer is: "an earnest request; humble entreaty made to God; devotional service consisting chiefly of praying; something prayed for." In Nelson's Illustrated Bible Handbook, "prayer is when someone can be totally honest with God...there is no need to pretend or mask emotions."

Because God's power is unlimited, the believer can have unlimited confidence in Him. No matter how grim the situation is, God can intervene. But, we have to be acceptable to God's purpose and plans that are best. This is where I, personally, have difficulty. We want what we think is best for us. I am guilty of that, aren't you?

There is such a thing as meaningless prayer: "I need a new car, and would you please have one by the curb in front of my house by morning; thanks, God, over and out." This is kind of extreme, but you get the idea, right? There is a huge difference between empty formality and true heart worship.

How many times have you said The Lord's Prayer? Thousands, right? But, to really pray it with meaning is entirely different. There are many prayers that serve as models for us to learn and study by. The empty repetition of these prayers in a vain hope of attracting God's attention or someone else by saying these prayers we've learned since childhood is not for any of us. We are free to come to God in prayer and be heard if we are *sincere*. Say these prayers we have learned with *deep* desire to be heard and a *loving* desire to get that close relationship with God.

God does not run us through some obstacle course of conditions before He hears us. Prayer is an expression of personal relationship. I can say these prayers I've learned since early on without much difficulty. Now, I'm sincerely trying to put meaning, my love for Jesus, and my commitment to God in these words I so easily spoke time and time again without thinking.

My problem is sometimes I just don't know what to say to God. Sometimes, I don't know how to begin. I've found, just like with any other relationship, I just talk to God. Not necessarily on my knees. I talk to Him while I'm driving, washing dishes, folding clothes, making beds, and working in my yard. I do this just like talking to a friend on phone. There is satisfaction, a glow that I feel after I have my little discussions with Him.

It's not the words you say; it is what you believe in your heart. To walk with God we have to learn how to have conversation with Him. Our normal situation around might not change—and then again, it might. It just makes me feel better when I have several good conversations with Him each day.

I've written so much about negative thoughts in this book. Praying can give you strength, courage, and peace to put one foot in front of another as your day goes on.

Prayer is opening our hearts and souls to God. One day I was getting bombarded with telemarketing phone calls. With just one glance at my caller ID box, I could tell when it was a telemarketer. There was just one call after the other with "number unavailable" displayed on the little screen. Annoyed, I said, "Lord, if I get one more of those calls, I'll pull the phone out of the wall!"

Well, He answered my prayer, alright. The electricity went out because of a thunderstorm and I didn't have anymore calls! It wasn't what I was really expecting, but He knew I was stressed and rushed that day. So with the electric off, I was not only assured of no telemarketing calls, I couldn't do anything else either until the electricity came back on. So, guess what it made me do? Yes, you are absolutely correct! It made me sit down and relax. It gave me time to unwind. I had to smile up at God and say, "Thanks."

I found a prayer that I have memorized. As I get up each morning I say this softly to myself as I start coffee, put the dogs outside to potty, before waking up family and things get hectic. It might help you too, so I'll pass it on. It goes like this:

Dear Lord,

I thank you for this day. I thank you for my being able to see and to hear this morning. I'm blessed because you are a forgiving God and an understanding God. You have done so much for me and you keep on blessing me. Forgive me this day for everything I might do, or say or think that will not be pleasing to you.

I ask now for your forgiveness. Please keep me safe from all danger and harm. Help me to start this day with a new attitude and plenty of gratitude. Let me make the best of each and every minute to clear my mind so that I can hear from you. Please broaden my mind that I can accept all things. Let me not whine and whimper over things I have no control over. And it's the best response when I'm pushed beyond my limits.

I know that when I can't pray, you listen to my heart. Continue to use me to do your will. Continue to bless me that I may be a blessing to others. Keep me strong that I may help the weak…Keep me uplifted that I may have words of encouragement for others. I pray for those that are lost and can't find their way. I pray for those that are misjudged and misunderstood. I pray for those who don't know you intimately.

But I thank you that I believe. I believe that God changes people and God changes things. I pray for all my sisters and brothers, and for each and every family member in their households. I pray for peace, love and joy in their homes that they are out of debt and all their needs are met. I pray that there will be no problem, circumstance, or situation greater than God. Every battle is in your hands for you to fight.

I pray all these things in Your blessed name, Jesus. **Amen**

8

♍ Pets ♎

Have you ever heard, "Happiness is a warm puppy?" Or seen the look on the face of a child when you place a little puppy or kitten in his arms? In Genesis 6:18-20, God was telling Noah to get into the ark with his family and get all animals, two of every kind. He expressed confidence that Noah would keep them alive. God gave us animals for so many different reasons: to help with labor, to help with transportation, and to provide companionship as pets.

Although God gave man dominion over animals, kindness to animals and laws concerning cruelty to them are seen several times in the Bible and in today's law enforcement. There are noteworthy scriptures in Numbers 22:22—23; 2 Samuel 8:4; 1 Chronicles 18:4; and 2 Chronicles 14:15. Additionally, Proverbs 12:10 states, "A righteous man regarded the life of his animal-beast."

In early Egyptian days, cats were held in very high honor. In more modern times, animals are frequently used in commercials and movies. For example, in Walt Disney movies, animals are constantly used as characters: *Beauty and the Beast; 101 Dalmatians,* the classic; *Ole Yeller; Oliver & Company; Rescuers Down Under;* and *Balto.* The list of movies goes on and on.

Dogs, in general, are used in every form of rescue and forensics. And sometimes, the dogs, themselves, need to be rescued. With the horrible Hurricane Katrina that hit the Gulf Mexico in the summer of 2005, people spent days upon days searching for lost pets, getting help for them, and reuniting them with their owners. The tearful reunions helped us appreciate how unconditionally our pets love us—and how much we love them back. That is an awesome love!

Animals were always a part of my life growing up. A cute memory I have of my brother, Steve, was when we were both small pre-school children living in Charleston, West Virginia. We had Beagle pups. Steve and I were young, maybe I was five and he was about two. Every time he tried to pick up one of the puppies, he would somehow manage to pick them up backwards. The puppy would be upside down, their little heads hanging down, their little butts up.

My mom would say, "No," and show him how to hold a puppy. After having received new instruction, Steve would lean over, apply his newly found knowledge—but somehow do it again. Heads down…bottoms in the air.…

Another incident occurred when we were older and living in Tennessee. It was around Christmas time. Steve came into our house one evening with this cute puppy wrapped inside his coat. (No, the puppy was not upside down this time.) Dad said, "No, no more animals." Steve was absolutely crushed. He headed for the door and went back outside. It was quite cold outside that evening. I think it had even been snowing earlier in the day. He was gone for nearly an hour, and I started to wonder where he was.

He must have walked around the block a number of times, thinking, because I'll never forget. I was there in the kitchen helping my mother with the evening meal. My brother walked in and pulled the same pup, again, out from his coat. He looked up at my mother and said, "Merry Christmas, Mommy. This is your present!" My mom looked at my dad. He shrugged his shoulders and nodded, "Ok." We named her, Phoebe.

How long it took my brother to think of that idea and how many times he must have walked around the block that evening I'll never know. But, I do know one thing: we were grown and gone when my brother came to my mom's house years later to see and help that same little puppy that was now old and dying. Phoebe died peacefully, wrapped in my brother's loving arms.

Animals can sense when a person is down or unhappy. I have dried many tears hugging the neck of a pet. I wonder if that's why God made them so soft and cuddly.

I have invested a lot of time, love, and veterinarian bills in animals. Recently one of our cats, Colette, died. The vet tried so hard to save her, but couldn't. I had her cremated so we could bring her home. Sounds crazy, huh?

You see, we cried and cried,—and I just couldn't leave her little dead body there. It's not like shopping for a new pair of shoes. You can't just say, "Ok, I'm willing to spend $100—and no more on healing this cat." Here's what happened. We took her to the vet's office. Colette was limp and unconscious. The nurse rushed her to the back room and started giving her I.V. fluids. After working on her for about 45 minutes, they said she was experiencing kidney failure, but there was a good possibility that they could save her.

With my grandson sitting there listening and agonizing through this with me, I was in quite a quandary. What was I supposed to say with my teary-eyed grandson looking at me? I considered saying, "No," but what came out of my mouth was, "Ok, try to save her." Five hundred dollars later, Colette died.

I have reaped so much joy from my animals. As you read earlier in one of my chapters, we have a new cocker spaniel. I also have a buff cocker named Diane.

Diane is about eight now. Well, she is *in love*. Yep, acting like a teenager. Thinks Ritchie, the Dennis the Menace dog, is the greatest thing with four legs. I haven't seen her act this frisky since she was a pup.

I often tell people I don't need to keep paying ADT Security, because the minute someone is near the house, my dogs all bark like crazy. The doorbell can ring on the television, and they all go barreling towards the front door.

So, gals when you are down and out, turn to that pet. They heal. They are teachers. They provide wonderful companionship. If you don't have one, get one. In most towns you can adopt a dog or cat through your local humane society.

Dogs are frequently taken to nursing homes to cheer up the elderly and to bring smiles and laughter to them. Animals are brought to patients who will not respond to anything or anyone else!

They have personally gotten me through many a hardship, their presence and unconditional love has helped me beyond measure. Do you know what we fail to do? Contribute their presence on this earth for us to our dear Lord.

Sometimes our pets leave us and go to heaven—or at least, that's what has always been told to me. This beautiful story goes like this:

> There is a bridge, called Rainbow Bridge, connecting Heaven and Earth. It is called that because it has many beautiful colors. Just this side of the bridge is a land full of grass, meadows, valleys, and places to romp and play. When our pets die, they go to this lovely land. There is always food, water, and grass. It is where old animals, frail animals, and even the young ones play and wait. There is only one thing missing: that special person who so dearly loved them on earth. So each day they run and play, eat, rest and sleep.
>
> Then one day, their noses twitch and their ears go up! They look around because they sense that familiar smell. Off they run!
>
> You take them in your arms and embrace them. Your face is kissed again and again. You look once more into the eyes of your trusting pet…your companion. Then together, you finish crossing the Rainbow Bridge on to Heaven, never to be separated again!

9

♍ Greatly Wronged ♎

Deep abiding friendships are very important to women. That's the way we are made. Deep within every woman's heart is the desire to connect with another individual. As we go through our stages in life, elementary school, high school, and college we meet many people. Some are acquaintances. Others are friendships that only last a short time, but have a wonderful impact on our lives. Their memories make us smile.

Friendship is one of the most powerful forces around. We go to high school and college reunions and get reacquainted with the people we once knew who touched our lives. The ones we had those giggles and slumber parties with. We look at each other and cannot believe the changes. We have all grown up and have kids; some of even have grandchildren.

As joyous as the anticipation of a reunion is, somewhere during the evening it becomes, in a way, almost sad. A reunion gives us a chance to talk and go back for a few hours to say, "Do you remember when we did…such and such?"

"Yes, but do you remember when we snuck out of the house that night and got caught, and our parents almost killed us?"

Or sad things like, "Did you know Frank got killed in Vietnam? He married Becky before he left, and she had twins. He never got to see them."

And there's always the "Oh, I'm sorry; heard you got a divorce." By the end of the evening, we've learned more about flaws and failures than about the new and exciting things happening in each of our present day lives.

I personally remember one incident from my high school days. One of my dear friends and I (with whom, 36 years later, we still keep in touch). We were at a dance that the school was giving. It was a Friday night. Diane had a boyfriend who was extremely possessive. Some other guy started flirting with her and before we knew it, a fight had broken out. Everyone was taking swings at each other.

This is a true story and I can honestly say that, just like the movies, a fist-fight can happen in a split second and the whole place is in shambles. I was on my hands and knees crawling between legs, trying to get the heck out of "Dodge". I had just about made it to the roped-off dancing area. I stood up to get over the rope and *splat whack!* I saw stars. I was out cold. One of the boys had accidentally hit me. He was swinging at someone else, and I was the lucky one, who got the sense knocked out of her!

Girls, have you ever wondered why guys do that? Why does the end result have to be fists? It has to be a man thing, guy-thing, or macho-thing. Those punches hurt! They must desire the taste of blood in their mouth.

And, "Oh, look at this shiner. Neat, hey?" It felt like I'd been hit with a golf club.

Well, needless to say, we were banned from coming back to the dances for the remainder of the year. We protested because it was the jealous boyfriend's fault. My parents took one look at me, I won't even go there. For weeks, I looked like a truck had run over me.

I wanted to hide at home, and not go to school. What would everyone say? Plus, I was so angry at my friend, Diane. It was her guy who started the fight. To this day, so many years later we still e-mail each other and talk about that silly dance.

What I am trying to get at is that friendships are so special. Things happen. Misunderstandings occur. You get them worked out and go on. Have you been greatly wronged? Or a person you thought would be there for you through thick and thin isn't. Harsh words may be said or written. One thing can lead to another, and eventually people who were the best of friends stop speaking. Tears may be shed to the point it gave you hick-ups. You make several attempts to mend fences with no avail. Your faith in the word "friend" gives you very serious doubts to its true meaning.

Then it hits you like a ton of bricks. I bared my soul to her for years. God maybe she wasn't the friend I thought after all. Then the anger festers and turns into resentment. Your stomach ties up in knots, and the joy slips out of your life. How could she do this to me?

And while I cherish the long-lasting and true friendship that Diane and I share, there are times when friendships end and leave you trying to figure out what happened. You are left with anger and resentment that can spread like cancer. If left untreated, it will creep into every aspect of your life. It will change you into a totally different person, and put a damper on everything around you.

None of us is faultless. And a good friend is not necessarily a perfect friend. Do we fall short? You can be certain we do. There is an old Turkish proverb that goes like this: "He who seeks a perfect friend remains without one."

There is a greater reason to forgive an individual who has wronged you. God commands us concerning forgiveness. Ephesians 4:31-32 "Get rid of bitterness, rage, and anger, brawling and slander, along with every form of malice. Be kind

and compassionate to one another, just as [God in Christ] God forgave you."
Luke 6:37 "Do not judge and you will not be judged. Do not condemn, and you
will not be condemned. Forgive, and you will be forgiven."

Loyalty is rare today. A loyal friend is worth his weight in gold. When you
think you've had just that, and wham! It is gone; the emotions can be so hurtful
and disillusioning. How do we cope and get through the pain? Again, pray, forgive. Turn it over to God.

A sign posted on a board in an office lounge said, "To err is human, and to forgive is not company policy!" Who would want to work for a company that never
forgave mistakes? Yet many people hang a sign on their hearts, "To err is human,
to forgive and remain friends is not my policy."

Criticism and judgment are two things that are deadly to any friendship. I
Corinthians 13:7 states, "Love bears up under anything and everything that
comes, is ever ready to believe the best of every person, its hopes are fadeless
under all circumstances, and it endures everything."

A positive friendship is based on a mutual understanding that we are human.
We all have frailties and shortcomings. We all make errors and mistakes—some
more glaring and obvious then others. As positive friends, we need to forgive one
another.

We need to assume the best about each other, not the worst. Half-truths and
assumptions often lead to death and destruction. Assumptions crashed the stock
market. False speculations have started wars, demolished reputations, and
brought things crashing down around you. Assumptions based on false judg-
ments caused an innocent man to die! That innocent man was Jesus Christ,
nailed to the cross.

Many of us find it difficult to forgive, especially when the offender is a friend
or family member. Sometimes we even blame God and wonder why He would
allow such an unfair event or circumstance to happen. I, for one, almost enjoyed
hanging on to an unforgiving spirit. Over time, an unforgiving spirit will rob us
of joy and peace.

I don't know about you, but I would guess that you've had to deal with hurts
and sadness. Under normal circumstances we have to deal with lots of things that
are not in our control. So, in cases where we have the right to control, I had to, as
the saying goes, "Let go and let God."

I prayed about the situation, and I forgave my friend (even though she is
unaware of this). It didn't happen overnight, but over time and months. God was
faithful, and the joy of the Lord resides in my heart that once was home to sadness and pain over the ending of this friendship with a woman I dearly held close
to my heart and cherished very much. I don't want you to think, "Oh, she makes
this sound so easy." It wasn't and it still isn't. It was painful, stressful, and tore at

my heart strings. We live in the same neighborhood. Our friendship lasted for numerous years.

We live in a fast-paced society. We are under great pressure to be our best, work our best, look our best, and feel our best…decorate our best. I can relate to this because I love my home and love to decorate. We have to buy the best. Mother the best. After we worked on being the best, we feel compelled to do basketball and soccer—and did I mention dance and voice lesson, then squeeze in church activities and, try to relax and have a cup of coffee with your neighbors.

So, when we have had the wonderful bond of a friendship and lost it, *ouch* it hurts and hurts badly. Women can understand each other in a way that men can't begin to even come close to. God is our designer and He created us, right? He completely knows us. He understands us better than any woman to woman conversations on earth. Yes, we can cry on our friend's shoulders, but we can also cry on God's shoulder. God is our perfect friend. God's friendship is our portion.

So, if some of what I have been through has happened to you, don't get discouraged. It is painful when a friendship comes to an end.

Have any of you ever been to camp? You know, like cheerleading camp or church camp? Or had a big bond fire at a local park and roasted marshmallows and sang songs? There was a song that we used to sing, *Make New Friends, but Keep the Old*. There was a phrase in it that says, "One is silver, but the other gold"

Well, my metal tarnished, and I was hurt; but with God's help and a lot of prayer, I believe I'll survive. There will be a scar there, and I'll always wonder why we couldn't have talked it out. As you know, with any relationship, it takes two.

I was at basketball practice one night waiting in the bleachers, like most moms for the kids to get done. One mom was telling me she has lived in her area for years and cannot tell you any of her neighbor's names. To me that is so sad! I feel so fortunate because I speak a lot to my neighbors and know most of them by name. We watch out for each other. Look after each other's homes and animals when one of us goes on vacation.

God wanted us to mingle, have those backyard barbeques and Fourth of July gatherings. We are getting so away from that sort of thing in our residential streets around this country. People don't want to be bothered or get involved. As long as we are in Satan's territory, the "world", he will try to attack us with indifference, shut the blinds and don't let anyone in, sort of attitude.

When 9-11 happened, it brought our country together for the first time in years. I am not telling you, you have to be like living in *Mayberry on the Andy Griffith Show* and run around bringing everyone cakes and cookies to their doors like Aunt Bea. Girls, there is a certain peace knowing I can call on one of my neighbors for help or just to talk. When my doorbell rings and it is one of my neighbors coming to see me, it is usually when I need a lift and God says, "Cindy, go ring her doorbell."

Or, I was walking down the street in late December when my neighbor asked me how my Christmas was? Little things in your neighborhood can make your day. It can be as simple as someone just driving by, honking and waving.

God intended for us, especially women, to have that closeness. In Genesis 1:26-27 "…view of mankind reflects a confidence that, with all our failings, we are special. We bear the image and likeness of God." This phrase "image and likeness" is best understood as a statement about personalities. We share with God capacities that only people possess: we think, we value, we choose. It is because we have, like God, a capacity for fellowship and meaningful relationships with each other.

It is a blessing to have friends that touch your life. It is an honor to have good neighbors. God's greatest gift to us women is that we have the capacity for love, self-sacrifice, appreciation for truth, beauty, and creativity. We are created in the image of God and "…we have infinite worth and value. Our respect for others, our acceptance, our sense of worth of every individual rests on this foundation." Psalms 8 and Hebrews 2:5-18.

So, if you have a very close friendship, cherish it! Acquaintances come and go, and they have meaning in our lives too. But have you ever given thought to just how many true friends will God actually bring your way in one lifetime? With so many unlimited long-distance phone services out there, cell phones, e-mail, and online chatting, you still can have together time separately. So, even if you and a friend are separated by miles, you can still be connected. Don't loose that special bonding called true friends. Taking these kindred spirits in one's life for granted is literally like taking a gift you receive,—let's say for your birthday—opening it, taking a look, shrugging, and then tossing it in the garbage.

10

♍ Do You Really Know the Person You Love? ♎

As women, when we fall in love,—whether it be the first time or not—we sincerely believe (or at least I did.) "Oh, my gosh! This guy has swept me off my feet. He is the best looking thing in pants. He is so *different* than other men I've met." Does any of this ring a bell?

The old saying, "Love is blind," in my case, was true time after time again. Not only was I blind, I was also stone deaf! I became hearing-impaired to advice given to me by friends and family. And as for God, I had completely shut Him out.

In retrospect, when I look back at my past relationships, see that I never once gave God the lead. God's vision for marriage is a place where we can be united as one. It is about sharing similar cultures, and similar likes and dislikes. It is a medium for us to grow and become what God intended us to become.

One of the most beautiful examples of this is our youth minister and his cute wife. They are an adorable couple, full of youth, just recently married. We are so fortunate to have them at our church; they are doing an awesome job.

We have a music ministry that will touch your heart. One Sunday, this young couple sang a duet. You could reach out and practically touch the love of the Lord that they had in their hearts, and the love they had for each other. It was almost as if a halo was wrapped around each of them, and God was standing behind them, just taking it all in. It touched me to my very soul and I told myself, "*That is a marriage blessed by God.*"

Sometimes, we rush into marriage without God's approval. We irresponsibly marry for different reasons: lust, to get away from our parents, or rebellion. Nine times out of ten, it never works.

How is this for being up front and honest: my relationships were disastrous and painful. And when the ill-fated relationships ended, the person who would be most damaged through it all would be the very person that I love more than anything, my daughter.

31

Of course, the more we have in common with the person we believe we are falling in love with, the more it works in our behalf. God provides the bedrock for shared values. It takes time and patience, and believe it or not, it also takes the *dating process* to achieve this goal. The utmost important issue, and where I have made my biggest errors in relationships, is literally not checking "them" out. I sound like I am purchasing a home or a car, don't I

I don't mean to be that un-feeling. At first, the infatuation makes you blind to sensible things. Love can hit us out of the blue, and we can meet Mr. Right who, we believe, is our soul mate. If it is true love and this hunk is your one and only, then he will be there and God will make sure you two are eventually united.

The pain you cause to yourself and to your children is too high a price to pay for making spur of the moment decisions like: "Oh, I just have to marry him now" Or, "If my parents say no, I'll run away and get married," or "I know it is love" when you have only met him a week ago! If these thoughts are going through your head, then hold on for dear life because it surely isn't God. It is Satan.

A good marriage or relationship becomes a place of shelter, hope, strength, communication, and friendship. Marrying swiftly or getting seriously involved without thinking, based on lust, or bubbling hormones may bring satisfaction, but only in the short run. Over time, that relationship that bought you so much pleasure can become a source of pain.

In 2 Corinthians 6:14 Paul says, "Do not be yoked together with unbelievers." Marriage is a partnership, and it is a lot of work and a lot of give and take. When you move into a serious relationship with such obstacles as different faiths and beliefs, and different levels of religious commitment, it can be really hard to make a go of it. The divorce rate in this country is sky high, and you may be adding to it if you don't reconcile such differences before marriage. When the going gets tough, it is far too easy to walk out, slam the door saying, "its over," and then just hire an attorney, and *poof* you are divorced.

When God says don't and we do it anyway, we are just asking for a dilemma of major proportions. My story goes like this: I was in a horrible relationship that was full of abusive behavior, yelling, and screaming. I realized I had a lot of questions about my life, and I knew I needed to make some tough decisions. Taking a trip to Florida was my answer. I would try to get my head on straight and reconsider my situation. I might even have some fun, soak up some sun, and enjoy the warm tropical breezes…the whole works.

Within a week or so, I was swept off my feet by one of the best looking men I had ever met. This guy was a real hunk. I mean, he was drop dead gorgeous! In my heart, I absolutely, positively knew that this time was *it!*

I don't know what I was thinking. I was supposed to be in Florida to get my thoughts together and figure out how I needed to handle my relationship back in Tennessee.

I had not given myself time to heal and do the right thing, and there I was falling for another man! And another thing is for sure: I had not stopped to turn to God for direction. After all, I didn't have time to stop—this guy was too gorgeous to resist! Remember, God's command not to be lustful is there for your own good.

Within a month, I brought this man home. I quickly got out of the abusive relationship and told everyone I had learned my lesson. I was absolutely sure that this new relationship was *it.*

Now let me stop here for a minute and say something: I really believe I did love him. People would tell us that they could look at us and see love written all over our faces. Many women, who have relationships with the wrong people, do love them. But, when in a mismatched relationship, they also miss so much of what God intended their marriage or relationship to be.

I returned to Florida, marrying him a few months later. Earlier, when I said for you to be patient…let God work…let their true colors shine through, I was dead serious. Foresight is less painful than hindsight.

God has forgiven me, but I still live with the consequences of this marriage every day. It turned out he was a liar, adulterating, and abusive alcoholic. Years later, I found out he was also a child molester. Yes, you read it correctly, a child molester, a monster!

Do you see what I am talking about? Satan is so strong and quick. Lustful actions are so deceiving. We are so blinded.

You are wondering what happened, right? The ironic thing is we were going to church and pretty involved in this church. I didn't understand it for years, but God was working for the best end-result. My husband had gone to the altar, accepted Christ, I thought. We had had some problems, but we seemed to be doing better. I believed things were looking up.

Now, remember, I still didn't know about the child-molesting. Where did I miss the warning signs? He was leading a double life. On the outside he was going to church and doing the right things. We had made it to our seventh year of marriage.

Then one day, out of the blue, he just upped and died. He came home from work, took a shower, lay on the bed…and died. He was 37 and he was dead suddenly in seven minutes!

It was horrible, shocking, and sudden. I was unprepared. I was 34 and devastated! Everything stopped! "He can't be dead! How could he be dead?" I screamed. I was puzzled. God! We were going to church, he accepted Christ as his savior. I thought things were just beginning to get good.

You know we are so sinful and so human. We just don't see the whole picture. God does work for the good in everything and He does see the whole sphere of things, when we don't. I know His heart was breaking at seeing me go through this anguish. If only I had just trusted Him to begin with…

The next five years, I can truly say were some of the roughest I've ever experienced! My teenage daughter went wild. Do you know why? My husband had molested her for years. She never told me because she knew I loved him and she didn't want to hurt me!!

She had a nervous breakdown. She rebelled against authority figures, and at the age of 18 was involved in a horrible car accident. To this day, I don't know how she survived.

I blame myself. It was all because I was selfish and not listening to God. I didn't just put myself in danger with abusive relationships; I also put my daughter in danger. Unwittingly, I positioned her to be hurt both physically and psychologically.

I had dysfunctional relationships, putting on wedding bands like changing shoes. My daughter has struggled with these issues for years. She in turn has had her own demons to fight as a result of her childhood with me. I am not a horrible person and I love my daughter. She always was well taken care of. We lived in fine houses, and had nice cars, furniture, and clothes. Yet, not listening to God's rules and not paying attention to His word can lead to heartaches that can ripple like throwing a pebble into water. The ripples go on and on and on and on regardless of whether you live in a shack or mansion.

I told you, when God says don't and we do it anyway, we are just asking for a dilemma of major proportions. It wasn't until several years later that the Lord maybe said to Himself, "She has had enough." "He" did lead me to a man with whom I spent nearly 20 years. The story of this relationship will be for another chapter later on.

♍︎♎︎

It's time for a commercial break and I'll be right back. I have to type this, though, while I'm thinking about it before taking a break by getting a cup of coffee and preparing for my daily routine. If I get one of my senior moments, I'll forget.

Writing this, my first book, doesn't come easy. These words just don't flow out from my mind spontaneously. I stop, think, and ask God, "Well, what do you want me to type next?" I get stumped and even quit for a few days. My mind shuts down. If I typed everything that has happened to me, I'd be typing for the next ten years and it would take you another ten years to read it.

So, I have to wait on the Holy Spirit to lead me. A lot of happenings in my life are important to me. Wonderful, exciting and I wish I could have all of you over to chat and have brunch. Wouldn't it be neat to exchange information?

There is a purpose in this, God has the lead and I am listening to Him and He is directing my thoughts. At times I can't seem to think of a thing to type and other times He puts so many thoughts in my head I have to literally say, "Slow down, God. I can't remember all this." Then I'll grab a pencil and start jotting down the ideas. One thing I am sure of: someone, somewhere out there has a need to read these certain experiences I have had. So for God's glory, it will help them either make the right decision, or at least tell themselves, "Boy, she really messed up. And look, she is still in one piece." I just don't know gals. If, with my experiences and mistakes, I can help, just one person, it will be well worth it.

11

♍ Flowers, Trees, Birds, and the Bees ♎

Everyone needs a good shot in the arm of Mother Nature. Back "in the day" when we started to bug our mothers during summer vacation time she would yell at us, point a finger at the door and say, "Out! Now! Go outside. Do something—just go outside!" That remedy still works today. When you are discouraged, down and out, and can't take anymore, here's a solution: get outside and commune with nature.

I recall saying in one of my past yearly Christmas letters:

> I don't have hobbies. I have passions. Gardening is one of my passions. When it is time to get out there and dig in the dirt is when I'm at my happiest. It's hard, sweaty, dirty work, and it pleases me to do it, year after year. For me, a garden is always a work in progress, never quite finished, and always a delight to the eye. At the end of a long day, whether it's gardening or dealing with a dozen chores that life hands out, there's nothing quite like a garden and a pretty yard to soothe the mind and the heart.

Not everyone likes to work in their yards, but what I'm trying to get at is this: God didn't intend us to sit around, sulking in self-pity. He doesn't want us to just close the blinds to life and sit in the darkness when you are down and depressed. Now, believe me, I know what it feels like. There have been times when all I want to do is bury my head like an ostrich. But when I start feeling that way, I rely on Psalms 16:11, "You will show me the path to life."

The path to life doesn't include shutting yourself away! It is getting out there. Get your bike out, walk, or jog. If you live near the ocean, go to the beach (but don't get involved with the good looking guy) and look at the massive waves and feel the presence of God. Sit on your patio or porch, and look around you at birds, trees, flowers, and bees. Smell the freshly-cut grass. Take a ride in the country, and look out at rolling farmland and all its beauty. Take a ride to the mountains. Get on a boat or ferry let that water spray on your face and touch, inhale, and feel God's presence in this universe. Walk down a rural road, and lean against a fence post. Maybe lean over and put a blade of grass in your mouth and feel the sun on your face.

The cold in your spirit will begin to thaw. A smile might even touch the corners of your mouth. A feeling of newness starts to seep in your bones. It might take several walks or several days of working in your yard or walking on the beach to feel your spirits lift—but do it!

Remember what I wrote earlier, my father died by a self-inflicted gun shot wound, in the darkness of a room closed off from God and nature and light and hope. The devil was right there watching him walk into the bedroom, cheering him on as he closed the blinds, helping hold the gun steady as the pistol went off, laughing as the bullet spewed out to end his life.

You are never alone. It is your choice whose company you want to keep: Satan's or God's. Jesus can calm the troubled waters when you are in dark despair. There is hope when you feel helpless. Just get out of the dark and into the light. Life holds so many precious things. The crushing pain of life is literally that, crushing. You must pick up the pieces and move on. Trials teach us lessons. The future is still out there despite our doubts and fears. Just hold on strong and don't let go. Take one day at a time.

Women, our crosses are hard to bear. It seems like darkness is everywhere, and troubles pile up around your door. You can choose to close yourself up inside and just wallow in self-pity. You can even get on the phone and call all your friends until you find someone who will feel sorry for you. Or you can take a deep breath, open the door, give your troubles a good kick, and hear your mom saying, "Out! Now! Go outside. Do something—just go outside!"

12

♍ Embrace Your Spirit ♎

The origin of this quote is unknown, but I absolutely love it: "If nothing ever changed, there'd be no butterflies." Butterflies represent the opportunities for growth, change, and transition. And like a butterfly, it takes courage to grow up and become the woman you truly meant to be. It takes courage to show the world you are different and unique. It takes courage to face your fears, but in the end you'll be happier and more fulfilled.

It took me years to realize that I don't have to have a man in my life to be fulfilled. I could do housework, mow the lawn, install a new doorknob, and pay the bills. I can also hold down a job, come home and do laundry while I cook dinner, then load everyone up to go back out to a band concert.

I have a toolbox that is mine. It has all the basics: a hammer, saw, screw drivers, and several wrenches. I actually bought a sander, electric drill, and an electric screwdriver. And girls, you can do it, too!

We can be multi-faceted. Sometimes it is tough. And I actually get disgusted because, at times, I had to call a male to come do stuff I just couldn't handle. It frustrated me and made me angry when I couldn't do simple things for myself. I tried to do many of the "manly" chores myself, and later had to tuck my pride and call someone to help. And that's just what you have to do sometime: just find a way to handle the situation! This is all a part of life—just deal with it!

The good thing about the "someone" that I called is this: I can send him home when he was finished. I didn't have to take any verbal or physical abuse; I didn't have to "put up with stuff" because I had no other alternatives.

There is always a way out with God, prayer, friends and family. 1 Corinthians 11:3-16 talks about understanding creation, principles, God, Christ, man, and woman. Additionally, it states, "woman is the glory of man." God never intended women to be a punching bag for men's hang-ups, insecurities, or jealousies. Life is too short to get caught up in such negative and unproductive emotions.

Be prepared. Get that trade, skill, or education that you've always wanted. Arm yourself with a set of skills that will enable you to live the type of lifestyle that you desire. Go to college, cosmetology school, and nail technician school, a technical college…whatever it takes. There are a thousand opportunities for women in this day and age today to earn training that enables them to support themselves.

Treat yourself like a queen. This is a reminder of just how royal you are. Step right up and joyfully claim your individuality.

My only regret is it took me so long to learn this lesson at my expense and the expense of others I loved, especially my daughter. That is why this book means so much to me. I'm reaching out to all of you. Don't wait until half your life is gone and then say, "Daah! Now, I get it!"

Create a self-fulfilling prophecy for yourself. You become what you think you are. If you think you are no better than sitting back and taking abuse, then that's exactly what will happen in your life.

It is so easy to dwell on negative thoughts. Instead, you must keep your mind filled with lots of positive affirmations. They will help you on your path to success. Continue believing in yourself. Set goals and systematically work towards them. Let your dreams take flight and don't let anything or anyone stop you.

Once you have achieved your dream of self-sufficiency, then, and only then, let the love of your life in—and only if *you* want it to happen. Imagine the harmony you will find when you actually have a lot to bring to the table. Imagine the strength you will feel when you know you don't have to be totally dependent upon someone else.

The Eagles released a song in the 60's called "Peaceful, Easy Feeling." Some of you may remember? There is a lot to be said about the song and what it stands for. There is nothing quite like a peaceful, easy feeling, knowing you are in control. God never intended us to be misused, abused or neglected. He created us and we are precious in His eyes.

Love is like playing the piano. First you must learn the rules of music, and next you must learn what each key can do. And as you develop your own style, you will be able to make beautiful music. And it is the same with love. First equip yourself with skills and education. Know what you are capable of. Know what you bring to the table. Then, you might be able to gain a sense of appreciation for a relationship that will let you play from your heart—by rules that you establish for yourself.

You've got to have faith. Patrick Overton said, "When we walk to the edge of all the light we have and take the step into the darkness of the unknown, we must believe that one of two things will happen. There will be something solid for us to stand on or we will be taught to fly." A set of skills will help establish that faith that you need in yourself. The knowledge that you are complete—with or without a mate,—will help you find the peace you need to let go of all that keeps you from being totally happy.

There was a plaque given to me once that had the ABC's of Life. Facts are neatly spelled out from A to Z like: "Accept Differences," "Be Kind," "Count Your Blessings," "Dream,"…"Yearn for Peace." I enjoy the plaque because it helps me focus on the positive.

There are so many ego boosters out there. If you have to purchase a dozen to put around your home or little inspirational saying magnets for the refrigerator, go for it. Just find ways to keep that positive attitude up!

The world is changing. It is up to us, for our sakes, if the change will be positive. Follow your ideas, your dreams, and your goals. Be guided by one of Mother Teresa's advices:

> "People are often unreasonable and self-centered. Forgive them anyway. If you are kind and people may accuse you of ulterior motive, be kind anyway. If you are honest and people may cheat you, be honest anyway. If you find happiness, people may be jealous. Be happy anyway. The good you do today may be forgotten. Do well anyway. Give the world the best you have, and it may be never enough. Give your best anyhow. For you see in the end, it is between you and God. It was never between you and them anyway."

13

♍ One Flaw in a Woman ♎

In Genesis 3:16, God talks about the worth of women. God strongly advises a woman to not have the tendency to make her relationship with her husband her primary reference point. If she does, the man might inadvertently or intentionally, rule her emotionally. In that case, her value, significance, and security would hinge on the man's response to her. When we marry, we often begin to put more emphasis on our relationship with our spouses than we do on our relationship with God. However, God wanted her deepest longings to hinge on Him this verse is actually the Achilles' heel for women. It can be her greatest stumbling block and the root of much of the dysfunctional behavior that women have in their relationships.

I have spoken about verbal abuse and how it hurts. It brings us down, and we start beginning to believe what is being said. James 1:23-25 reads…purity of life is not a quest for perfection as much as a quest for liberation from those things that may inhibit effectiveness and reduce joy, happiness, and a power-filled living."

In James 1:26, God talks about the tongue and how we cannot have control over our lives unless we control it. Women, we are worth so much. Don't—don't let anyone tell you differently. When angry tongues start wagging, feelings tend to get hurt.

The tongue has slain more people than all the armies that have marched on earth. The tongue has implanted doubt, fear, and discouragement into many lives. Homes, families, and friendships have all been destroyed because someone did not think before they spoke.

The real damage is done in the mind first. Maybe in an emotional outburst—or perhaps simply out of apathy—words filled with anger, resentment, and insensitivity spurt without forethought. So think carefully before you utter those words that you can never take back.

Let no one demean you. God's deepest longing is to have you turn to Him. He knows your worth. When your self-esteem is starting to deflate, lean on God. Remember your worth.

One Flaw in a Woman

Veronica Stone (excerpt) Women have strengths that amaze men.
They bear hardships and they carry burdens,
But they hold happiness, love and joy.
They smile when they want to scream.
They sing when they want to cry.
They cry when they are happy
And laugh when they are nervous.
They fight for what they believe in.
They stand up to injustice.
They don't take "no" for an answer
When they believe there is a better solution.
They go without so their family can have.
They go to the doctor with a frightened friend.
They love unconditionally.
They cry when their children excel
And cheer when their friends get awards.
They are happy when they hear about
A birth or a wedding.
Their hearts break when a friend dies.
They grieve at the loss of a family member,
Yet they are strong when they
Think there is no strength left.
They know that a hug and a kiss
Can heal a broken heart.
Women come in all shapes, sizes and colors.
They'll drive, fly, walk, run or e-mail you
To show how much they care about you.
The heart of a woman is what
Makes the world keep turning.
They bring joy, hope and love.
They have compassion and ideas.
They give moral support to their
Family and friends.
Women have vital things to say
And everything to give.
However, if there is one flaw in women,
It is that they forget their worth.

14

♍ More Rape Victims Speak Up ♎

How much can you accomplish in an hour? Read three chapters of a book? Make a pan of lasagna? Wash two loads of clothes? Deal with the fact that 78 women just got raped—and that one out of every seven of those women will have been raped by her husband? Sadly enough, however, only about 16 percent of rapes are ever reported (statistics from the Coalition Educating about Sexual Endangerment).

Scott Berkowitz founded the Rape, Abuse, and Incest National Network (RAINN), the largest anti-sex-assault organization in the country. According to Mr. Berkowitz, the reporting rates are actually rising. He credited the increase in reporting to increased public awareness and public policies that are tougher on crime.

An additional element that has directly affected the increase is us: a generation of women who have grown up with "no means no." "In the past, the reason people didn't report was that they feared nothing would be done, or that they wouldn't be believed, or that it was too personal a crime," said Jamie Zwieback, spokesperson for the Rape, Abuse, and Incest National Network in Washington, D.C. "People are starting to realize that it will be taken seriously."

I was blessed to have had people in my life that cared enough about me to say, "Get help." Others would say, "If you are emotionally out of balance, then everything you say or do is going to be out of balance." So I took their advice. I went to counseling. I joined women's groups. I began to read books and magazines about other women and how they dealt with having been raped.

Through listening to many women, both friends and acquaintances, share their stories of pain, I began to understand. I began the healing process.

I heard stories that fit the stranger definition of rape, and I heard stories about women who were raped by men they knew and trusted. All these women were rape survivors. For women, rape is one of the biggest issues in their lives; however, for some men it can be reduced to a joke.

We live in a culture that almost seems to condone violence against women—and even rape. Maybe I am simply more sensitive to it, but it seems like every other movie on television has some type of violent sexual scene.

While traveling once, I stayed at a hotel where there happened to be a bunch of drunken men. One guy yelled, "We'll rape whoever we want…Come to our rooms so we can rape you." They were laughing the whole time. Then they turned and did that male macho kind of thing where they punch each other's backs and shoulders.

Rape is the silent epidemic of our society, the hate crime never spoken about. I hope that the women who have been sexually assaulted have the courage to talk with someone. Until men stop raping women, there can never be true equality between the sexes. No issue better represents the power that men hold over women than rape. We are not a free society when half the population is afraid to walk alone at night.

While I am typing this paragraph, at least three women have been raped. But it seems like more men care about the game on Sunday than the fact that millions of women have been the victims of rape or attempted rape.

In Webster's dictionary, the meaning of rape is: (1). the crime of having sexual intercourse with a woman or girl forcibly and without her consent, (2). the act of seizing and carrying away by force, and (3). ravish, violate.

Ravish. Violate. Those words are terrifying to any woman—even one who has never remotely experienced a man taking them by force. You feel so utterly filthy. No amount of bathing or scrubbing can remove the disgust you feel inside and out. No amount self-talk can clear your mind of what has just happened to you. No amount of time can ever completely heal the scars of having been ravished, of having been violated.

Through all of that, however, if you remember nothing else, remember this: *you* are the victim. It isn't your fault. Those are the things that sustained me and gave me unbelievable strength even though my own personal nightmare happened years ago.

My very real disappointment was with the judicial system at the time. As the "incident" made its way through the system, it got ugly. I still remember the comments, snide remarks, the threats, and oh, the looks. If those looks could have killed, I'd be dead. If I were not a stronger woman, I would have retracted my statement and just given up. After all, I didn't ask to be violated. I was an attractive woman who just happened to be in the wrong place at the absolute wrong time.

Since the beginning of time, women have been plagued by the male ego and lust. In 1 Peter 2:11, Paul begs man to put fleshy lusts away because they bring war against the soul. Paul speaks strongly of lewdness. He calls it "unashamed actions, unbridled lust." Psalms 14:3 states, "They have all turned aside, they have together become corrupt; there is none who does well, no not one." In Genesis 34:2 we are told "...and when Shechem the son of Hamor the Hivite, prince of the country saw her, he took her and lay with her, and violated her." Judges 19:25 speaks of assault: "They knew her and abused her all the night until the morning."

Just remember: what goes around comes around. The rapist will get his just rewards. So in my case, where I did not receive the justice I deserved, these words, counseling, and praying for strength helped pull me through this horrific situation.

Gals, like everything else I have written in this book: hold your head up high. Get back to living life to the fullest. With God as my witness, it isn't easy. It was hell. Over time, the pain physically and mentally healed. It became clearer to me about my pathway: I must bow to the pain and open my heart.

Hidden on the other side of pain is universal love and acceptance of myself and others. There is something extraordinary in my capacity to survive. I must trust in the struggle. I must write this book so others can heal. As I committed myself to healing, I was led to a deeper understanding of myself. The essence of finding the meaning to what happened to me was not to forget my experience with rape, but, instead, to remember it.

To move forward, you must embrace your past. All of your experiences—good and bad—have helped to shape who you are today. Somewhere along the way, I read: "Listen to the music of your past. For it is in listening to the music of the past that you can sing in the present and dance into the future."

15

♍ You Have the Right to Say, "No! ♎

One of the cornerstones for creating a life you love is setting limits. Before you can set limits with other people, you have to set boundaries for yourself and stick to them. You have to feel down to your soul and heart what is and isn't acceptable to you. You have to know your bottom line, and then you must enforce it. Breaking the bad habit of permitting you to be mentally or physically abused it starts with desire, is fueled by courage, and ends with discipline.

One of the toughest, or should I say, most challenging obstacles I had to overcome was learning to say, "No." I had to learn to set limits. I had to learn to enforce the boundaries regarding what—and who—I was willing to accept in my life.

It is scary, I know, when you are up against an aggressive, rude, yelling, foul-mouthed individual. It is hard to look that person in the eye and say, "This is enough. I won't take this anymore. You are not going to treat me like this!"

For me, there was a period of trial and error. The first time was probably the scariest. And in the first several incidents, I didn't come out on the winning side. I was still developing my style of "defense". I was still learning what to say. Kenny Rogers gives perfect advice in his song: "You got to know when to hold them; you got to know when to fold them, know when to walk away, and know when to run."

Each time you get stronger and stronger. I hit a turning point, maybe close to my fortieth birthday, when I developed a backbone. I guess as I got older, I also began to get wiser.

Listen, I'm not telling you to sit there and get yourself harmed. Hitting back physically isn't the answer, either. That is the purpose of dialing 9-1-1. Some of our abuse is verbal, and it is up to you whether or not—or just how long—you are going to take it. At some point, ladies, you have to fight back! You have to stand up for yourself. If you don't, it only gets worse.

Listen to your feelings. Recognizing that anger and resentment can be purposeful. That's a tall order, especially for us females, considering that in our culture, women are considered selfless. Anger often signals that you aren't getting your needs met, or that you are overextended. Your feelings of frustration and resentment, which are anger's cousins, let you know that you've compromised or sacrificed too much of yourself. The choice is yours. You can use your feelings to become more motivated or you can simply sit there and feel sorry for yourself.

You do not have to live like that! Leave. Go stay with a friend, a neighbor, or at a women's shelter. I learned to say strongly and with conviction, not loud, but firmly, looking them, my abuser, directly in the eye, "Your behavior is unacceptable. I do not have to listen to this. I can't change you; you have to change yourself. I do not have to stay. I am leaving, and we'll discuss this reasonably later when you aren't acting like a nut case."

And I'd leave. Sometimes I would just go to the other side of the house; other times I would go outside, go for a walk, or get in my vehicle and drive off.

The first time I did this, I thought I'd never make it out of the door. I was so afraid. I tried to look courageous as I walked away. It was hard not to look back. It was even harder not to go back.

I think I put him in shock. He just stood there with his tongue hanging out of his head. He wasn't sure what to think—and I wasn't either. When it worked, I felt like jumping in the air.

The physical and mental pain can be grueling not just to you, but to everyone who loves you. It can be tragic to anyone who depends on you for strength and guidance. Remember my daughter?

But the benefits to your health and to your attitude can be priceless. I still have nightmares about things that happened to me during those years when I just stood there and took it. Courage is a door that can only be opened from the inside. Harry Truman said, "Imperfect action is better then perfect inaction."

The woman I have become today didn't happen over night. I kept trying those "imperfect" actions. And you, too, can break free. If you are going to live a high-quality life, you have to have healthy "self-protectiveness". You must find a balance between the needs of others and your own.

Henry Ford had another phrase I admire: "Whether you think you can, or think you can't…you're right." How do you find your individual courage? There are no easy answers. Search your soul. Pray. Ask God for strength. But most of all, find your reason.

Ask yourself: "Do I want to go on like this? Do I want to continue living like this?" Deep down inside yourself you know the answer, right? Then you will be unstoppable.

One of the obstacles you will run into, especially if you are in an abusive relationship, is this: the person that is closest to you doesn't want you to change. He wants everything to remain the same. Your "mate" doesn't want you to set limits, and he certainly isn't going to help you do it!

There is a certain amount of comfort to be found in that which is familiar. In most cases, your abusive mate is scared. He is afraid of losing your presence, and he is terrified of losing your love. He might really, really love you, but it is a distorted love…a sick love, and by no means the healthy love that you deserve.

To paraphrase Helen Reddy's song: "We are women, hear us roar." We all have doubts, fears, and disappointments. Setting boundaries will no doubt cause you to quake in your boots. When you set limits, feelings of doubt, fear, and being unsure of yourself will be well worth the effort. Why? Because when you set and maintain your boundaries, you will become a healthy and happier person.

Ask yourself who could make a positive difference in your life when faced with difficult choices or challenges. To whom could you turn for guidance? For me, I was thinking of a friend, family member, or pastor. For you, it might be someone totally different. The answer might not come to you immediately. Just think about it for a while.

Lean on the Lord, and lean hard. He will give you strength that is unbelievable! He provides an inner peace that is so calming; it is almost like being lulled to sleep. Remember the old adage: "nothing ventured, nothing gained." So, go ahead. Venture into God's arms and just see what you gain.

I have no idea who the author is, but there's another quote that I like, "The measure of a truly great man is the courtesy with which he treats lesser men." From a woman's point of view, it should read, "The measure of a great man is the courtesy with which he treats a woman."

And with that in mind, I will end this chapter with another fabulous thought by Ellen Sue Stern, "Long term change requires looking honestly at our lives and realizing that it's nice to be needed, but not at the expense of our health, our happiness, and our sanity."

16

♍ Our Sexuality ♎

Now it's time for the "s" word: sexuality. I've purposely chosen not to discuss it so far in this book because my main purpose, until now, has been to encourage women to stand on their own two feet, set limits, and refuse to be "man handled."

But that is only part of my dream for you. The other part is for you to realize your potential as a woman now—not to wait until half your life is over, then wake up and smell the roses, so-to-speak.

God created the beauties around us: the earth, heavens, animals, plant life, and the sea. Then He declared that it was good. Next, He created a man, but decided that something was missing. The man needed a help mate. So God took a rib from the man's side, and created a woman. The woman's role was to be a helpmate to the man.

Nowhere in the Bible have I read that man and woman were made to just live happily ever after in total accord, agreeing on everything, holding hands and blissfully skipping through the fig trees. Even Adam and Eve had an argument— you remember the apple thing, right?

Sometimes couples will disagree. Sometime couples will argue and have misunderstandings. No two people can live together 24–7 without some type of conflict. What I want you to remember is that there is a huge difference in a little couple's "spat" or misunderstanding, and in sacrificing your physical and mental health by letting a man abuse you.

We women have the power to make or break a man. Many times, women tend to forget the power they hold in a man-woman relationship. A word of encouragement or a tender touch can make a man feel ten feet tall and ready to conquer the world. And yet, just as easily, a nagging word and a cool attitude can make him feel like a total failure.

We women can play a key role note in regards to the men in our lives. This is where I want to emphatically stress: this is a dangerous game to play. Regardless if the marriage is quote-un-quote reasonably "normal" or if you are going through an abusive relationship, don't use your sexuality as leverage. Don't use sex to get control.

With this mental-physical tug of war, many men turn to other women or become outraged. When they become outraged, well, you know what can happen—it can lead to resentment. Resentment can lead to abuse.

By withholding sex and love, women might temporarily get their way. But in the long run, this is a dangerous weapon to use against a man. I know I might be sounding a bit chauvinistic, but I'm just trying to tell you that this "holding back" won't stop the abuse and holding back won't make your relationship better if that is what you're striving for.

Sulking, getting mad, and withdrawing our sexuality is not the way to build a healthy relationship. And it is definitely not a way to handle someone who is verbally or physically abusive.

A relationship is more than a 50-50 proposition. It is a 100 % proposition from each partner; and each one is working and striving for a harmonious relationship in the home. And harmony at home flows out into our daily activities.

Sex is fulfilling and comforting—it is that special time when a man and a woman come together as one. Tensions are relieved, pressures and cares are forgotten, and love is deepened. With love comes faith, trust, and belief in each other.

We, as women, must think positively. When a woman gets her head on straight, she will realize her body is not a bargaining tool. Her true status is to become the woman she is meant to be, not by using that sexuality to get her way or to punish, but by striving towards a goal she has set for herself and then reaching it. A real woman will use her God-given beauty and true self to encourage and inspire. She will use her sexuality to bring happiness, love, and a little extra "spice" to that certain person in her life.

17

♍ Social Relatedness and Respect ♎

How do I approach the subject of partiality and prejudices without stepping on toes? Whoever is holding this book now and reading it, I can not expect for them all to be Caucasian! Abuse, verbal or mental doesn't stop only on the white woman's doorstep. It is everywhere, in every walk of life, in every race.

Human beings possess a relationship to one another and to God that no other creature does. James 2:1-9 suggests that to be human is to experience a multitude of social relationships. The Bible doesn't say that certain races are created in God's image; instead, it says man was created in His image. Additionally, Genesis 1:26 tell us that "all human beings have an equal value and, by their humanity, are interrelated."

For so many years, there was a lot of anger and ignorance stemming out of sheer prejudice regarding mixed relationships. But God, in James 2: 1-9 says, "Human worth cannot be valued by ethnicity, wealth, social standing or educational levels, because all are significant and valuable in God's order."

From a Christian standpoint, to regard race, group, or any individual as less important than another is sin. Let us learn to respect and honor every person regardless of his station or color. Our impartial God shows to all people the same love, grace, blessings, and benefits of His salvation.

The abusive behavior is not limited to one type of race of people; it affects us whether we are Christians, Jewish, Catholic, or Islamic. No woman deserves to be hit, taken advantage of, or put in a compromising position—no matter *who* the man is. God would not tolerate it and neither should we.

I live in a military town where mixed marriages and relationships are a common sight. The neighborhood in which I reside has approximately 40 % mixed homeowners. We all live together in harmony where no one thinks twice about our differences.

Living in the south-eastern part of the USA, You still run into your stick-in-the-mud, opinionated citizens who resort to using slang terminology for the Negro, Mexican, Chinese, Vietnamese, and Korean races. We all have human worth. We all bleed the same way and die the same way: when our heart stops!

My next-door neighbor, who happens to be a Black man, has been sick a lot this winter. Does his hurts and pain register any less because he is African American? There is an Asian couple that lives around the corner. They take walks around the area frequently, holding hands. By watching them, you become very aware of their closeness and love. Do they love less or more because they are of a different color or race or religion?

Then you have rumors or stories you've heard for years like African American men like to hit their women, or according to rumor, all Germans are Nazi's and all Mexican men will slit a woman's throat without thinking. We hear that the Islamic people hate Americans because of the war in Iraq. The list of rumors and stereotypes goes on and on.

These types of statements are so one-sided, and are based on sheer ignorance. There are good and bad people in every race. In my life, I have heard some pretty bad hypocritical statements from people who I never would have believed would come out of their mouths.

We live in the "land of the free" where opportunities are out there for everyone, but we can't get past prejudices. Does the good Lord look down on us and shake his head? Probably?

18

♍ Be Kind ♎

In Acts 28:2 the Bible talks about kindness, love for mankind, hospitality, readiness to help, human friendship, benevolence, and consideration for others. The word is a compound of *philos*, meaning love, and *anthropos*, meaning man. In Titus 3:4 philanthropia is used to describe God's loving, kindness toward men.

Another excellent verse on this subject is Galatians 5:22 which says, "But the fruit of the spirit is love, joy, peace, longsuffering, kindness, goodness, faithfulness." To me, it means goodness in action, having a sweet disposition, and being gentle in dealing with others. The 23rd verse of Galatians talks about gentleness and self-control.

Kindness is the ability to act for the welfare of those taxing our patience. It is easy to be kind to people we like, but to be kind to an individual we do not like is an entirely different story.

If today were the last day of your life, what things would you do? Who would you make sure you speak to? How would you treat people? William Penn wrote, "I expect to pass through this life but once, if therefore, there can be any kindness I can show, or any good thing I can do to any fellow being, let me do it, for I shall not return this way again."

Kindness is an attitude of serving and caring for others. Human connection and demonstrating acts of kindness is so important! I see and help create acts of kindness on a daily basis. When you're stuck in traffic, and someone lets you into their lane, give them a wave or honk to say, "Thank you." In a grocery store when *your* shopping cart is full of food and the person behind you only has a few items, let that person get in line in front of you.

Humility is not an act, but an attitude. One day my mother had been trying to call, on and off, with no luck getting in touch with me. It was a combination of me not retrieving my voicemail and Thomas my grandson not picking up on call waiting. She was concerned because I had been sick and she wanted to know if I was ok. The kindness of my mother was showing through as she repeatedly tried to contact me. When we finally connected, I assured her I was getting better. Out of respect, I apologized, "Mom, I'm sorry. I didn't mean to worry you."

Humility is a magnetic force that attracts goodwill from people, and it honors those who possess it.

I have a big jar in my den that I put all of my coins in each day. The coins come in handy because I use them to pay for those spur of the moment things like car washes, the ice cream man, and tips. At one point, my jar had about $10 in it. So when I had ordered pizza one evening, a young lady delivered it. I had already paid for the pizza by credit card, but I wanted to give the lady a tip. I told her to hold out her hand because her tip was mostly coins.

Somewhere in the process, she recognized my name. She said she had heard about my husband's death, and offered her condolences. Believe it or not, instead of taking the tip, she tried to give *me* money! I kept saying, "No, no!"

As we continued to talk, she shared her own personal story about something that had happened to her. In 2003, there was a house fire. In the disaster, she not only lost one child, she lost three!

We talked for a while longer, and as she headed for the door, she told me her name was Liz. We swapped telephone numbers and promised to keep in touch. She told me if I needed to talk, to just call her. She said that people were so good to her when her tragedy happened that she wanted to return the kindness to me. We have talked a few times, and each time I felt blessed to have met her. I felt thankful for her acts of kindness and compassion.

Those who achieve humility and kindness usually are blessed beyond their wildest dreams. To lose patience and say something hurtful or sarcastic seems so easily done in this day and age. Sometimes, we fail to think of the consequences of what we might say or do. But there are others who delight in misleading, embarrassing, and making people squirm in discomfort.

Do you believe acts of kindness are showing your weakness? Maybe you are afraid. You've heard all sorts of stories about people who followed God, who put their trust in Him. You don't want to become a religious fanatic, right? We have drives, and they are either good or evil. They are simply part of human nature, and being human we tend to lean towards the path of least resistance. As you lean, make sure that the path you are taking is one that will produce results that you can feel good about.

Somewhere, years ago, I read about a man who wrote a book in which he said the most important thing on earth was to be number one. On the dedication page of his book Robert Ringer wrote, "Dedicated to the hope that somewhere in our universe there exists a civilization where inhabitants possess sole dominion over their own lives." Well! There *is* such a place. It's called Hell. It is a place where men have totally divorced themselves from God's claim on their lives.

In Gatlinburg, Tennessee several years ago a man by the name of Ben Hooper stood up and told his story. His mother wasn't married and Ben had a hard time.

When he started school, the boys had a name for his mother, and it wasn't a very nice name. What was worse was when he went downtown on Saturday nights feeling every eye was burning a hole through him as they wondered who his father was.

He used to go off by himself at recess because of the taunts of his classmates cut so deeply. When he was twelve, a new preacher came to his church. Ben always came late and slipped out early. But one day, the preacher said the benediction so fast that Ben was caught going out with the crowd.

Just about the time he got to the door, the preacher laid his hand on Ben's shoulder and said, "Who are you, boy, and who's boy are you?" Ben felt the old weight come on him. It was like a big, black cloud. Even the new preacher was putting him down. But as the preacher looked down at him, studying his face, he began to smile a smile of recognition. "Wait a minute, he said, "I know who you are. I see the family resemblance. You are a son of God!" With that, the preacher slapped Ben across the rump and said, "Boy, you have a great inheritance. Go and claim it."

That was the most positive, kind statement ever said to Ben. On two occasions, the people of Tennessee elected an illegitimate child to be their governor—one of those occasions was when they elected Ben Hooper.

At all costs, try real hard to be kind to the people you meet on a daily basis. Christian life is never free from mistakes. The best of us spend time in the ditches of life.

As a woman who has made her share of mistakes, I spend a lot of time pulling over to the side and saying to friends and strangers who are in the ditch, "Though you have fallen, you still can get up and start again. Come on, give me your hand. I'll help."

Jesus was a perfect man. He was kind, tender, gentle, patient, and full of love and that is what He demands of us. John 14:23 reminds us: "If you love me, you will obey my command." Be kind, tender, gentle, patient and full of love. Remember, kind words can make a person's day—or ruin it. Which would you want to be responsible for?

19

♍ Christmas Letter 2004 ♎

When you are trying to put together thoughts and words to pass along to friends and relatives this time of year, when most of our energy is being put on trimming the tree, baking, church activities,…shopping how does one tell or break the news in a Christmas letter that is suppose to be filled with happiness & joy that things here at the Lilly residence are just not quite right?

I regret to inform each of you that my husband is battling cancer, and has been, since he was diagnosed this past summer. As his caretaker and his wife, I can say but one thing—this man is a fighter!

He has gone through emergency surgery to reinforce his femur bone in his right hip that the cancer was destroying and he has gone through radiation. He is still going through chemotherapy intravenously and orally.

A few weeks ago he had to have a blood transfusion. We are constantly fighting low blood counts, anemia, nausea, and a thousand and one things associated with this disease. One being, my husband has lost close to 80 lbs!

One good piece of news came to us, and is a wonderful Christmas present and a miracle from God: the cancer has *shrunk* in his lungs. We take one day at a time and that is all we can do.

Cherish each moment we have together? You bet! Giving up hope? Nope! Have people praying for us and getting prayer chains going? Yes!

Having friends and family calling, caring, and being there for us is overwhelming. My wonderful Mom in Tennessee calls almost on a daily basis.

Sometimes does the Lord let this kind of thing happen to bring us to our knees? Possibly? Humble us? Maybe?

I have been able to share 20 years with Richard, us celebrating 18 years of marriage this past November. He is my husband, my friend, and has been my soul supporter for all these years.

He has taken a baby into his household (Thomas) and raised him as his own. These two are incredibly close and Thomas is trying to cope with his daddy's sickness as best as he can.

Richard is a good man, not a perfect man or easy man, but the hardest working man I've ever seen.

We have overcome many hurdles together, and our wish as we approach this joyous season is to have each of you continued to pray for us. Pray to give Richard strength to continue his battle with this cancer. Pray to give me the strength to be there for him and by his side.

And above all, believe in miracles. A miracle happened over 2000 years ago with the birth of our Jesus. Can I not believe that a miracle could happen, and that Richard and I could enjoy many more years together? Or that he could watch a young boy, who calls him "daddy" grow into adulthood? Believe in miracles.

20

♍ 20 Years with Mr. Right ♎

After all that I've been through, after all that I've had to work so hard to overcome, how could I possibly begin to say good-bye to the one man that God undoubtedly sent to me to help make me complete? How do I let go?

How do I help my friends and my neighbors understand that the "old" Alana is also gone? How do I help them redefine their image of me—a new woman who is missing a vital part of her?

It takes so much courage and support to go on—to face each new day. You wake each morning after having tossed and turned all night. You roll over to the spot where he is supposed to be in bed, waiting to feel his body bump against yours. You drag one leg off the bed, and try to force yourself to pull the other onto the floor. After all, you have to start your day, right? You have to go on.

And that's where God comes in. When you are crying so hard you get the hiccups, He is there. When you finally get the courage to go through his closet, He helps you get through the pain as you sort, fold, and put everything in boxes. And when Father's Day and Christmas comes for the first time—without his presence—God is there to remind you that people are mortal, and they will come and go in your life. But through it all, you will survive. You can go on. Just look to the hills from which comes your help.

♍♎

Please Understand

A tribute to Richard who died April 12, 2005

There it is down in black & white.
What I mean is, he's still alive in spirit, but his body died.
And that's how I became a member of the community of the bereaved.
And as a member, I ask for your understanding.
Not your pity, your understanding.

As individuals, we in this community of the bereaved need you.
Don't worry about saying the "right things."
We're tired of clichés.
We know our dear ones are "at peace" with God and that they feel no more
pain.
But, right now it doesn't help.

But we still miss their physical presence.
There was one person on earth to whom we were the most important
They supported us, spoiled us, took care of us financially,
Argued with us, were very unreasonable,
At times-did their "man thing" which went against our nature and was like a
piece of chalk going down a blackboard and irritating our nerves.
The one person who knew us so completely that no words were necessary.
Held us. Kissed us.
We miss that. And so much more!

If we seem distant, please understand.
Some of us are still in shock.
Even if the illness was long and the prognosis unfavorable,
We maintained our normal routine: around the house, the yard, shopping,
Taking kids to school and school functions, caring for that loved one
Just hoping that death wouldn't come.
We had to!
How else could we face each hour and encourage our loved one to keep their
chin up and try to maintain their strength by eating anything we come up with
to help their appetite?

Then failing and feeling miserable because they took a few bites and turned
away or didn't want it at all.
The weight loss. Oh, the weight loss. And the pain.
It seemed nothing helped.
In their last days they drift between two worlds.
How else could we keep our sanity?
Hospice. The gratitude of Hospice. Those people are wonderful.
Those nurses who care for the dying.

A nurse or midwife coaches birthing and
Helps bring a life from the womb.
At the other end of life a Hospice nurse helps ease the transition
From life through death.
We gain an insight and understanding you need to find something good in the
sadness and pain of losing someone you care about.
The wonderful book *Final Gifts* those richly told stories enable us to come to
some kind of peace.
We discover the wisdom, faith, and love that the dying leaves us.

If we seemed angry or selfish, or foolish or childish, please understand. Most of
us were angry, foolish, selfish, and goofy.
But we know now that God accepts our anger, fears, and foolishness
And refines it into an energy that will be vital in our days, weeks and months
ahead as we grieve, deal with the pain and grow stronger.

If tears come at inappropriate times and places,
If we get panicky, please understand.
There is no shame in tears.
Weeping cleanses the heart of sadness and refreshes the soul.
In 1 John 11, Jesus was so distraught over Lazarus's death,
Who was one of His dear friends, He wept along with Lazarus' family.
You see Jesus was in human form and cried!
Our emotions, even yet, are raw.
Just when we think we are in control, a song or scent or a piece of clothing, a
restaurant, a place or a feeling of utter desolation overcomes us.

Or if we laugh or cry one minute, and laugh the next, wail the next,
Do all these things at inappropriate times and places.
Know that deep inside we are hurting.
We know that God has given us the gift of emotions,

a sense of humor and that our loved ones are rejoicing that we are exercising these gifts.
Some of you may think we are "losing it" as the saying goes.
We're not. It is called shock.
It's what happens now? What will I do without him? Is he really gone?
How will I pay bills? How does this or that work?

We may be forgetful—a lot of time we are. It is like living in a fog.
Sleep is elusive, while our loved ones were ill
Now that they are gone, it's even worse.
We may not eat properly.
We may make foolish purchases, silly spur-of-the-moment decisions.
Please don't condemn us.
Just know it is part of the grieving process.
In time, we'll come around.

The Greek word for love is *"agape*
The Hawaiian word for hello and welcome is *aloha*
The Hawaiian word for good-bye and thank you and God speed is *mahalo*
The biblical meaning of "love" is defined for all time by Jesus' self sacrifice on Calvary.
Being loved by God was only the beginning.
God plants love within our personality.
Dear friends, let us love one another,
For love comes from God who has given us the only "real" shoulder
To lean on in our grief process.
With our grief comes another fellow that likes to
Kick us while we are down: Satan
He loves when he wins.

Death and Satan's hand brings strange things out in our friends.
Some shun us, some misjudge us, and some turn their backs on us.
Dear friends, let us love one another.
For love and forgiveness comes from God.
Friends, since God loved us, we also ought to love one another.

Don't hide behind flimsy excuses.
If we love each other, God lives in us and His love is complete in us.
Love for one another is only possible because of Jesus.
Then we have friends that stick by us like glue and truly surprise us.

The ones we thought would be there, weren't (which we have found, in our
community of bereaved, is very normal)
We still love you and forgive you and welcome you back into our lives
The door is always open.
It's never too late to say, "I'm sorry."
The Holy Spirit will press upon our hearts to say,
"Get thee behind me, Satan"
and give you and me the ability to love, forgive, put the past behind us, and love
as Jesus loves us.
Only then can you find peace.

The ones we thought were just acquaintances or not as close come out of the
woodwork and bless us beyond anything we could imagine.
A miracle happens and you meet a church and church people who welcome you
with open arms.
Then the Lord takes our broken spirits and our broken hearts and our pain and
our grieving and leads us down the path of new friendships and new beginnings.
What a privilege to share with others the love that God has lavished on us! And
what a model of selfless love we have in our Lord.
Life is full of surprises, thank goodness!
We can't move forward while looking backward.
We can't spend our lives looking over our shoulders, asking "why" and "what if."
We look forward to our future and embrace new people and new challenges
head on.

And please, oh please, let us follows our own timetables.
We each march or stumble along this route at our own pace.
Grief has no calendar. Don't hold us to a timetable.
For the moment, we are drifting, buoyed by the love of God.
Big emotional crashes are like car wrecks.
Don't expect to walk away unscathed, and don't expect to heal overnight.
We'll be okay, but it will take time to recover.

This faith, along with your understanding, will enable us, eventually, to cele-
brate life once again.
My goals are to relax more, be sillier more, limber up, take one day at a time,
travel more, and see different places.
Oh, I've had my moments and if I had to do it over again,
I'd have "more" of them. In fact, I'd try to have nothing else.
Just moments, one after another, instead of living so many years ahead each day.

♍♎

And for you, dearest Richard,
I will carry you in my heart forever!
You would make me so angry at times with your stubborn Marine Corps
embedded personality.
Oh! You had the heart of gold!
Hard on the outside and so loving and caring and giving on the inside.
The nearly 20 years with you was definitely a journey and not one of always
bliss!

But love you, cherish you, yes!
The love you had for us was so unselfish and so giving.
You are truly missed my dear husband.
I love you.
You are truly missed, dear man!
Until we meet again one day, I vow I will not hide my love from people.
I resolve to help my friends in need of support.
I am strong and I can grow from pain.
I intend to live my life to the fullest.
My time is precious.
I have learned that nothing is more important than our faith in God, our
church family, our dearest friends, our family, and our health.

With much love and hope for your understanding,

Your wife,
Alana

21

♍ Christmas Letter 2005 ♎

I sit here with a cup of coffee at my computer desk looking outside on this chilly morning (only 26 degrees!) with the sun streaming in my den window here in Jacksonville, NC.

I am trying to get my thoughts together to form my yearly Christmas and New Year's letter. I find myself being rather scatter-brained this holiday season. Starting one project after another, attempting to get myself in the mood. It is like my mind is detached from the festive surroundings with my body just somehow going through the motions.

I've always enjoyed sitting down and composing this, sending the news to all—good or bad. As Christmas Eve approaches this, by far, is the most difficult correspondence I've tried to compose and send off.

A few days ago, I told myself that I just wouldn't do one this year. I discovered since, however, that these letters bring people enjoyment, smiles, tears and amusement. So that puts me on a guilt trip, so-to-speak. On this cold morning, bear with me, and I'll try...

For friends and family out there who do know, please be patient with me while I sadly break the news to those who don't know. In my last Christmas letter of 2004, I stated that Richard had cancer, and we were fighting this battle very hard.

Well, April 12th, my husband died and went on to be with our Lord. Cancer has a terrible way of creeping up and winning. With the sadness of loosing someone you love, with grief that on some days just won't let go, I know he is in a better place. No more pain, no more suffering.

Thomas and I are still struggling, after eight months, to get our heads and hearts to cooperate. Our heads tells us he is in heaven and so much happier, but—and that is a huge but—our hearts are selfish and we miss him terribly!

Marriage is such an up and down, trial and error relationship. Believe me, Richard and I had our share of all of the above. He was no angel and, of course, neither was I. Richard was, undoubtedly, the most warm-hearted pig-headed, giving, and caring person I have ever met.

He spoiled me rotten and drove me crazy, calling me a thousand times a day. Do you know what? That is what I miss the most: his voice and his calling me so often.

I am so proud to say he was my husband for nearly 20 years. The love he had for Thomas and I shone through occasion upon occasion, year after year.

I am still astounded, even though he is physically not here, how even in death, his loves goes on in my memories and the way he arranged to take care of Thomas and me.

He will be truly missed as this festive season draws near. This Christmas he is spending it with Jesus.

The people left behind are dealing and coping. Especially, Thomas and I, the best we can for with all these *firsts* without him: his birthday, which was in August, Thanksgiving, Christmas, etc. We continue on, knowing that one day we will meet again. So each of you, as you read this, stop a minute and say a little prayer for us as we face Christmas alone without him.

I can honestly say I am looking forward to the New Year. Last year was so difficult. Now, maybe, with the grace of God, as 2006 approaches, we all can breathe in some fresh new beginnings. Maybe we can laugh more. Maybe we can cry less.

I can have hope that things will work out for the best. Thomas will grow as independent as possible, carrying his memories of daddy with him everywhere he goes. He will tuck all he learned from him in his heart and use it to the betterment of his young future.

22

♍ The Shock of Death ♎

Sometimes an experience changes us forever. Your life falls apart, you move numbly in slow motion.

It was the loneliest, most bereft moment of my life when Richard died. At 9:00 A.M. on April 12th, he had no blood pressure. There was no pulse. Eleven hours later, he was still barely hanging on…barely alive. He was so close to death.

I could barely breathe because I was now so tuned into his condition. For nearly eleven hours, I lay next to his dying body. Breathing in and breathing out. In. Out. His rising and falling chest, the only thing keeping him alive.

The Hospice nurses saying he was fighting like a tiger with some inner something that was a pure miracle. With no blood pressure and pulse, now going on eleven hours, my husband did not want to leave me. He didn't want to leave Thomas.

Soothingly, I whispered in his ear most of the day. Reassuring him it was ok to go. I would miss him. We all would. But, I had to let him go. At nine, an hour later, his hand slipped from mine. My husband died.

I felt his soul leave his body. And as *we* became *me*, my heart shattered into twenty million pieces.

He had been so ill, and now he had no more pain and suffering. I took one day at a time. One foot in front of the other. Sunrise. Sunset. I couldn't, wouldn't, cry. I was absolutely afraid to cry. I thought if I started, I would not be able to stop. Somehow, my tears would be like throwing in the towel, signaling, yes, Richard is dead!

During countless, grief-stricken nights, I sat up to the early hours of the morning with tears streaming down my face. The tears came without my permission. They came in spite of my objections.

Ten months later there are a couple of things I know for sure: in this world, good is stronger than evil and love is stronger than hate.

My husband's soul survives, and his memory lingers on. I take everlasting comfort in that. Through death, through wars, even through sorrow and pain, peace starts to creep in. Like a plant, it starts to grow and flowers again.

We can't control life. Things change. Life is about changing. No one knows from minute to minute when our last breath will be. When death strikes, we want to strike back and strike back hard! We are selfish and want our loved ones back. Acknowledging that we are now in an arena, in which we have no control, makes it harder.

When the peace and healing comes. And, gradually, it will, cherish it! Savor it. Honor it. Cling to it. It is God's way of wrapping His arms around you. It is His way of whispering in your ear saying, "Everything is going to be ok. You know I am here for you." He will walk with you, prodding you to keep going, "Keep moving, my dear. You have got to go on." And as loneliness and doubt creep in, He will remind you that you are never alone. "Don't worry; I'll hold your hand every step of the way."

Losing a loved on, watching your husband die, or ending a marriage or relationship in which you had great hopes, future plans, and thousands of memories—both good and bad—can all deal out the same emotional turmoil. They can all feel the same as they end: terribly gut-wrenching.

The crushing pain of life is literally that. *Crushing*. You feel as if you are at your wits end. You wonder if it's possible to go on. You're afraid to try to find out what's on the road ahead. You must know, however, that the *bend* in the road is not the *end* of the road, unless you refuse to take the turn.

You have to pick up the pieces and move on. Trials teach us lessons. The future is still out there despite our doubts and fears. Just hold on strong and don't let go. Take one day at a time.

23

♍ The Obituary ♎

Master Gunnery Sergeant Richard L. Lilly USMC (Retired)

Born: 25 August 25, 1934

Richard is preceded in death by his first wife Barbara A. Nary Lilly and father William Floyd Lilly. He is survived by his wife Alana L Lilly; his mother, Flossie P. Gross, and his sisters, Brenda of Colorado, Sandra of Mexico, and Diane of Washington State; two sons, James Randall Lilly of Texas and Thomas Michael Maynard of Jacksonville; daughter, Pamela Carol Lilly of Jacksonville, NC; stepdaughter Tessa Morgan of Tennessee; granddaughter, Victoria Maynard; ten grandchildren and four great-grandchildren as well as many loving and devoted friends.

Richard Lilly joined the US Marine Corps 25 August 25, 1951, after attending Beckley High School, Beckley, West Virginia. Corporal Lilly served in Korea with 5th Fifth Marines, January 1953 to June 1954 as a radio operator. Sergeant Lilly was assigned to Tenth10th Marines, 2nd Second Marine Division, and Camp Lejeune for 18 Eighteen months until May 1955, when he was sent to Inspector-Instructor Staff, Evansville, Indiana where he was promoted to Staff Sergeant. SSgt Lilly was the Noncommissioned Officer in Charge (NCOIC) for Toys for Tots and assisted with March of Dimes campaign as well as several other types of community services. After attending the Radio Chiefs Course in San Diego, Staff Sergeant Lilly returned to Camp Lejeune assigned to 3rd Third Battalion, 8th Eighth Marines; Headquarters, 2d Second Maine Division and 6th Sixth Marines. In August 1960 he went to recruiter's school. While assigned as the NCOIC at Marine Corps Recruiting Substation in Pikeville, Kentucky, Staff Sergeant Lilly was Recruiter of the Year 1962 for 5th Fifth Marine Corps District. He did three tours in Okinawa: November 1962 to November 1963; 1967--68 and August 1973--1974. Master Sergeant Lilly served in Vietnam as a Communications Chief in 1968--1969. He was promoted to Master Gunnery

Sergeant (MGySgt) in 1970 in San Diego, California while attending the Communications Chief Course. He returned to Camp Lejeune and was the Regimental and Division Communications Chief with 8th Eighth Marines; Headquarters 2nd Second Marine Division and Headquarters Force Troops, 2nd Second Force Service Support Group (FSSG) until he retired in 1977 after 25 twenty-five years, 8 eight months and 26 twenty-six days of exemplary service. During his time in service MGySgt Lilly received the following commendations and awards:

Navy & Marine Corps Commendation Medal V
Combat Action Ribbon
Navy Presidential Unit Citation
Joint Meritorious Unit Award
Marine Corps Good Conduct Medal (9 awards)
National Defense Service Medal
Korean Service Medal
Vietnam Service Medal
United Nations Medals
Republic of Vietnam Campaign Medal
Republic of Korea Presidential Unit Citation
Vietnam Gallantry Cross Unit Citation with Palm and Frame
Republic of Vietnam Campaign Medal with Device

Richard settled in Jacksonville, NC. after retirement [from the Marine Corps], he worked as a courier for First Citizens Bank then for UPS while building a real estate business. He has been a wonderful asset to the community often donating time and money to many charities as well as books and other needed items to local schools.

Funeral Services will be held Saturday, April 16, at 2:00 PM at Jones Funeral Home Chapel with the Reverend Robert Hall and Steve Pross. Interment will follow at Onslow Memorial Park.

To those of us who have had the honor and privilege of being a part of Richard Lilly's life, we shall miss this dear man more then he could ever imagine. Go rest high on that mountain, Richard. Go with God!

While the family will greatly appreciate flowers they would like to ask you consider carrying on Richard's desires to help the community by donating to either the Richard L. Lilly Scholarship for the Survivors of Cancer Patients or to the Onslow County/Jacksonville Special Olympics. Thank you and God Bless!

Family will receive friends Friday, April 15, at Jones Funeral Home in Jacksonville, North Carolina from 6:00 until 8:00 PM.

24

♍ Now, I'm "The Widow" ♎

As I learned and accepted the fact that I was a widow, I did not instinctively know what to do or how to be coping with my grief. I reached out to people who had walked that path before me. I learned that to ultimately heal, I must touch and be touched by the experiences of those who had gone before me.

These people offered me hope, inner strength, and the gift of love. The secret of healing in grief and accepting that I am now my husband's widow was the love and support of people who surrounded me with compassion. This love was the antidote to my pain. It was the acceptance of this love, after Richard died, that helped me with the desire to go on living.

I realized, very simply, that if I wanted to live again, I must seek support, understanding, and guidance. Being lost, scared, and confused didn't mean I had to stay that way.

Part of healing and being Richard Lilly's widow was to express myself publicly again. It took courage, self-love, and determination to move from the inward position of necessary retreat to the outward position of necessary risk. Yet, to venture out enhanced my ability to live again the way I wanted to.

I had never known pain quite like this before. It overwhelmed me. Even now, I am adapting and growing. I am entitled to be proud of my progress. As my grief changes, I reflect on where I have been and where I am going. Working on my grief, I guess, could be called "soul work."

Death caused me to become more intimate with myself, with others, and with the world around me. This journey has definitely been an education. It has had major disappointments, numerous eye openings, and many hurtful experiences.

Today, I am more spiritual and deeply connected to my higher power. Learning to adapt to becoming a widow, I discovered that life and living are sacred, beautiful gifts to be treasured each and every moment. The pain of death, losing someone you love, and becoming the "widow" taught me about the gift of loving and being loved.

The death of my husband may be one of the greatest pains I had to endure. I had a rough life, and God sent Richard to me as a reward for making it thorough so many troubles. I could hear him say, "Well, done, my good and faithful servant…"

Death signifies the end of what I have known that made me feel safe. I sometimes feel overwhelmed by the fear of an uncertain future. Will I ever love and be loved like that again?

There, are so many people out there that will literally tell you anything to take advantage of the vulnerability of your recent situation—especially if money involved.

People that you haven't seen in decades will suddenly come out of the woodwork! Then there are people who have "always admired you from afar." In what seems like minutes, they profess their undying love for you.

Be careful. Move slowly. Believe me when I tell you, men will say anything to get money or sex. Don't fall for it because it is very painful and you don't need that kind of let down after such a great emotional loss like the ending of a relationship or the death of a loved one.

The death of someone I loved made me examine where I am right now, today, as his widow. His death came without my permission. While I realize death is universal, it was hard for me to contemplate the death of someone who brought meaning to my life.

Death and loss creates the obvious: living without the presence of someone loved. Learning to survive my changed life forces me to draw upon all of my resources. The active cultivation of my changed self helps me discover a new depth, beauty, and richness in my life.

As I learn to nurture my new self, I find new appreciation for each new day, each new relationship. The more I come to understand the new me, the more I have to give back to my life and those I love.

Discovering my changed me" clears a space to discover new life. I have something to turn toward instead of away from. I have something to cry out for that releases my inner tension. I have something that is authentic, real: it is the life that breaks through my loneliness, with direction and power of its own.

25

♍ Read Only if You Have Time for God ♎

When I read something that inspires me, I hold on to it. As things happen in my life, I often dig through my files and piles of inspirational quotes and messages until I find one that suits the occasion.

I don't have any idea where this came from. It was probably one of that e-mail's that came forwarded to me from someone to whom it had been forwarded, and that person received it from someone who it had also been forwarded to.

Read Only if You Have Time for God

God, when I received this, I thought to myself, "I don't have time for this." and, "...this is really inappropriate during work" because I received it on the job.

This e-mail.

Then, I realized that this kind of thinking is exactly what has caused lots of the problems in our world today.

We try to keep God in church on Sunday morning...and maybe, Sunday night...and, we might include Him in the unlikely event of a midweek service. We do like to have Him around during sickness...and, of course, at funerals. However, we don't have time, or room, for Him during work or play because that's the part of our lives we think we can, and should, handle on our own.

May God forgive me for ever thinking that there is a time or place where He is not to be first in my life?

73

26

♍ Placement ♎

As we contemplate loss and moving on, we sometimes search for meaning and placement. Yes, placement. We make decisions about where God ought to be.

Where in this situation does God best fit? Where, in this situation, can He be used to help me? You've done it: "Oh, I'm afraid or worried," so I need to pray. "I need God to intervene in this situation," so I need to pray.

But when life is good and things are going smoothly, it can be quite easy to become less dependent on the very God who has helped you through all of the "bad" stuff.

Learn to consistently lean on God, and as Proverbs 3:5 encourages us, "…lean not on your own understanding; in all your ways acknowledge Him, and He will make your paths straight."

Make your pile. Create your file. Those inspirational articles, quotes, and notes can be your "place to go" when you need to be uplifted, when you need a reminder of just how wonderful you are, when others are depending on you for inspiration and support,—or when you need to reconsider *placement*. Take time for yourself. Take time for God. ♍♎

Poem

(source: unknown)

I knelt to pray but not for long,
I had too much to do.
I had to hurry and get to work
For bills would soon be due.

So I knelt and said a hurried prayer,
And jumped up off my knees.
My Christian duty was now done
My soul could rest at ease.

All day long I had no time
To spread a word of cheer.
No time to speak of Christ to friends,
They'd laugh at me, I'd fear.

No time, no time, too much to do,
That was my constant cry,
No time to give to souls in need
But at last the time, the time to die.

I went before the Lord, I came,
I stood with downcast eyes.
For in his hands God held a book;
It was the book of life.

God looked into his book and said
"Your name I cannot find.
I once was going to write it down…
But never found the time."

27

♍ Memories ♎

Memories may be good or bad or in between, but in all cases, they seek to be embraced. Each memory can be savored as unique, reflecting how the person impacted your life.

By understanding the preciousness of memories, I can embrace the way I live my life. I have the privilege to seize each moment, to live until I too, die. Embracing memories of those who die helps me understand the true value of time. I must remember to let others know I love and cherish them as gifts from God.

My memories, especially those that imprinted my heart, stay with me forever. My five senses have taken in my memories and made them a part of me. They are always available to my inner mind.

My capacity to love and be loved makes my heart fertile with memories and images; these images cannot be pushed away. My memories are an affair of my heart. Some fresh and warm. Others painful and not so pleasant.

Without a doubt, my continued living is connected to my heartfelt memories. Remembering the person I have loved allows me to slowly heal. Healing does not mean I will forget. Actually, it means I will remember. Gently, I will move forward, never forgetting my past, but longing to return to the world around me.

As I reflect on memories, I discover a depth of meaning even in the simplest of events. Memories allow me to care for my heart. As I remember those I have loved, I realize I will never tire of embracing the same events over and over again. For only through reviewing what was, can I create what is, and what will be.

Memories are my treasures. They carry my story, my song, and my light. As I long for peace, I carry my memory torch with me, a vital link in the chain of humanity.

28

♍ Closure ♎

We, as women, are so blessed. Life is so very promising, especially when we stay on course, walking steadily on the road revealed by God. We are blessed when we follow his directions. Go down the road He set.

As I read the eleventh chapter of Luke, I am reminded: no one lights a lamp, then hides it in a drawer. It is put on a lamp stand or a dresser so those entering the room have light to see where they are going. Your eye is a lamp, lighting up your whole body. If you live wide-eyed in wonder and belief, your body fills up with light. Keep your eyes open, your lamp burning. Keep your life as well lit as your best-lit room.

As I close this book, I hope you will find just one or two things to put in your pile or in your file. From time to time, re-read the sections that can have a positive impact on whatever is happening in your life. Use this book as a tool—no use it more like you might use a recipe book.

When life becomes stagnant, look up the "recipe" for something new, something different. Add a little spice to your life. Using a recipe book doesn't mean you don't know how to cook. It simply means you want to make a better meal.

As you re-define yourself and your relationships, I pray you will learn to love appropriately. Use your head. Test your feelings. Get to know yourself. Give love sincerely and with intelligence. Remember me, and learn from my mistakes.

I leave you with Philippians 1:9: "And this is my prayer: that your love may abound more and more in knowledge and depth of insight."

29

♍ Statistics ♎

1   Nearly one-third of American women (31 percent) report being physically or sexually abused by a husband or boyfriend at some point in their lives.
—Commonwealth Fund Survey, 1998

2   It is estimated that 503,485 women are stalked by an intimate partner each year in the United States.
—National Institute of Justice, July 2000

3   Estimates range from 960,000 incidents of violence against a current or former spouse, boyfriend, or girlfriend each year to 4 million women who are physically abused by their husbands or live-in partners each year.
—Violence by Intimates: Analysis of Data on Crimes by Current or Former Spouses, Boyfriends, and Girlfriends, U.S. Department of Justice, March 1998

4   Studies show that child abuse occurs in 30-60 % of family violence cases that involve families with children.
—"The overlap between child maltreatment and woman battering." J.L. Edleson, Violence against Women, February 1999

5   While women are less likely than men to be victims of violent crimes overall, women are 5 to 8 times more likely than men to be victimized by an intimate partner.
—Violence by Intimates: Analysis of Data on Crimes by Current or Former Spouses, Boyfriends, and Girlfriends, U.S. Department of Justice, March 1998

6 Violence by an intimate partner accounts for about 21 % of violent crime experienced by women and about 2 % of the violence experienced by men.
—Violence by Intimates: Analysis of Data on Crimes by Current or Former Spouses, Boyfriends, and Girlfriends, U.S. Department of Justice, March 1998

7 In 92 % of all domestic violence incidents, crimes are committed by men against women.
—Violence against Women, Bureau of Justice Statistics, U.S. Department of Justice, January 1994

8 Of women who reported being raped and/or physically assaulted since the age of 18, three quarters (76 percent) were victimized by a current or former husband, cohabitating partner, date or boyfriend.
—Prevalence Incidence and Consequences of Violence against Women: Findings from the National Violence against Women Survey, U.S. Department of Justice, November 1998

9 In 1994, women separated from their spouses had a victimization rate 1 1/2 times higher than separated men, divorced men, or divorced women.
—Sex Differences in Violent Victimization, 1994, U.S. Department of Justice, September 1997

10 In 1996, among all female murder victims in the U.S., 30 % were slain by their husbands or boyfriends.
—Uniform Crime Reports of the U.S. 1996, Federal Bureau of Investigation, 1996

11 31,260 women were murdered by an intimate from 1976–1996.
—Violence by Intimates: Analysis of Data on Crimes by Current or Former Spouses, Boyfriends, and Girlfriends, U.S. Department of Justice, March 1998

12 A child's exposure to the father abusing the mother is the strongest risk factor for transmitting violent behavior from one generation to the next.

—*Report of the American Psychological Association Presidential Task Force on Violence and the Family, APA, 1996*

13 Females accounted for 39 % of the hospital emergency department visits for violence-related injuries in 1994 but 84 % of the persons treated for injuries inflicted by intimates.

—*Violence by Intimates: Analysis of Data on Crimes by Current or Former Spouses, Boyfriends, and Girlfriends, U.S. Department of Justice, March 1998*

14 Family violence costs the nation from $5 to $10 billion annually in medical expenses, police and court costs, shelters and foster care, sick leave, absenteeism, and non-productivity.

—*Medical News, American Medical Association, January 1992*

15 Husbands and boyfriends commit 13,000 acts of violence against women in the workplace every year.

—*Violence and Theft in the Workplace, U.S. Department of Justice, July 1994*

16 One in five female high school students reports being physically or sexually abused by a dating partner.

—*Massachusetts Youth Risk Behavior Survey (YRBS), August 2001*

978-0-595-38787-8
0-595-38787-X

Printed in the United States
220046BV00003B/32/A